DAVID E. JOHNSTON
editor

Discovering
Roman Britain

contributors
ILID ANTHONY
JAMES DYER
LESLIE GRINSELL
DAVID E. JOHNSTON
BARRY M. MARSDEN
EDWARD SAMMES

SHIRE PUBLICATIONS LTD

Contents

British Library Cataloguing in Publication Data: Discovering Roman Britain. - 2Rev. ed. - (Discovering Books; No. 272). I. Johnston, David E. II. Series. 936. 104. ISBN 0-7478-0212-2.

Cover: *Late first-century black and white pavements in the north wing at Fishbourne palace, West Sussex.*

ACKNOWLEDGEMENTS
   The cover photograph is by David Baker. The maps and plans were drawn by Robert Dizon. Other illustrations are acknowledged as follows: Colchester and Essex Museum, plate 10; O. G. S. Crawford (from *Wessex from the Air*), plate 10; James Dyer, plate 46; David E. Johnston, plates 4, 9, 17, 18, 19, 21, 22, 23, 26, 28, 53, 58, 60, 61, 65; Cadbury Lamb, plates 4, 7, 8, 11, 20, 24, 25, 27, 31, 32, 36, 37, 38, 41, 43, 44, 47, 48, 49, 50, 51, 55, 56, 57, 59; Tony Rook, plate 15; the Société Jersiaise, plate 64 (photograph E. F. Guiton); Totem High Rise Photography, Colchester, plate 14 (courtesy of the Colchester Archaeological Trust).

Printed in Great Britain by CIT Printing Services, Press Buildings, Merlins Bridge, Haverfordwest, Dyfed SA61 1XF.

Preface

This book grew out of a suggestion that the Roman entries in the series of books *Discovering Regional Archaeology* should be amalgamated to form a new book. But this is more than a reincarnation of old texts: for each author has revisited each site, rewritten the entries and added new ones. The result is an entirely new, comprehensive visitors' guide to Roman Britain.

The authorship is as follows: Dr Ilid Anthony, *Wales*; Mr James Dyer, *The Cotswolds and Upper Thames, Eastern England, Wessex* (jointly with Mr Grinsell) (i.e. part of Avon, Berkshire, Buckinghamshire, Cambridgeshire, Essex, Gloucestershire, Hertfordshire, Lincolnshire, Norfolk, Oxfordshire, Wiltshire); Mr Leslie Grinsell, *South-western England, Wessex* (jointly with Mr Dyer) (i.e. part of Avon, Cornwall, Devon, Dorset, Somerset); Mr Barry M. Marsden, *Central England, North-eastern England, North-western England* (i.e. Cheshire, Cleveland, Cumbria, Derbyshire, Durham, Hereford and Worcester, Humberside, Lancashire, Leicestershire, Greater Manchester, Northamptonshire, Northumberland, Shropshire, Staffordshire, Tyne and Wear, Warwickshire, North and West Yorkshire, and Hadrian's Wall); Mr Edward Sammes, *South-eastern England* (i.e. Hampshire, Isle of Wight, Kent, Greater London, Surrey, East and West Sussex). The introductory chapters (1 to 6), Scotland and the Channel Islands are by Mr David E. Johnston. County boundaries are as in 1993.

For this second edition all entries have been checked and revised by the Editor. Many sites have been revisited and suggestions from reviewers and readers gratefully incorporated. The advance of research and improvements in conservation over the last ten years have enabled us to withdraw a few sites and add several new ones that are now worth visiting. Notable losses through closure are (at the time of writing) Keynsham (Avon, 2), and Reading Museum. We must hope that they will reopen during the lifetime of this book.

1. *The Britons submitting to Claudius: an engraving from the 1774 edition of Temple Sydney's 'New and Complete History of England'.*

1. Introduction

Anybody living in Britain some twenty years, let us say, on either side of that fateful day in AD 43 when the Romans began their conquest of the country will have watched with amazement and no doubt profound misgivings the transformation of his native land. Only yesterday, he might have mused, we were proud and free: today we are a conquered people. Fifty years later, the historian Tacitus tells us, the results of Romanisation were everywhere to be seen: 'temples, public squares and private houses ... so the Britons were gradually led on to the amenities that make vice agreeable — arcades, baths and sumptuous banquets. They spoke of such novelties as "civilisation" when really they were only a feature of enslavement.' The twentieth-century visitor who uses this present volume diligently may well feel that Tacitus is giving us only half the picture; what fuller picture of Roman Britain can the archaeologists construct for us?

It is fashionable in some quarters today to maintain that the Roman conquest changed nothing fundamentally. This may be true, by and large, for those who lived in the highland settlements of the Welsh or Cornish mountains, or in *Caledonia*, where the coin in your hand was a curiosity rather than an item of currency, bearing the image of an emperor who meant nothing to you; where the only 'Roman' you might ever see would be the tax collector, a Briton like yourself even when dignified by the title of *conductor*, or imperial agent. Even the Cotswold shepherd, in full view of his employer's villa, would have seen his colleagues cultivating the fields and harvesting the crops in ways that had changed little over the centuries. Today, crossing an empty field and picking up a sherd of Roman pottery, one is tempted to wonder: was the Roman occupation merely a passing phase in the history of Britain?

In fact, the predominantly Celtic character of the Romano-British landscape has posed a problem for us in choosing sites. Our readers will naturally wish to be directed to those that are visibly 'Roman' in character. But perhaps we should direct them to the hut circles and field systems that are admittedly Roman in date but purely prehistoric in character, or even to sites where important finds have been made but nothing is visible? We have compromised on this, believing that the best-preserved sites are generally the most rewarding but accepting that we may be distorting the image of Roman Britain.

It is hard not to see this image through twentieth-century eyes. Stand, for instance, on Hadrian's Wall and look north. Ask yourself: which side of the wall would I rather have lived? In the distance are the native hillforts and Roman marching camps that speak of centuries of resistance to Roman rule, and where the advanced frontier of the Antonine Wall lasted little more than twenty years. Behind lay the security of the Roman province, and all that the *pax Romana* offered. The symbol of this is that tax gatherer, for Rome offered, or rather imposed upon her subject people, a kind of business deal. Rome was to provide security, above all: security from invasion, from tribal and civil war, from personal enslavement, from widespread economic disaster, from anarchy and lawlessness. We shall see presently that every one of these guarantees was valueless in the end; but for some four centuries Rome kept her side of the bargain, on the whole. The physical legacy was the monuments that we describe below; the inheritors were new peoples, bringing with them a new language, new laws, new gods. A 'phase' in British history had indeed passed. But four hundred years of Roman rule had nevertheless left their mark.

2. Historical outline

There are three fallacies about Roman Britain with which we have all, to some extent, been brought up: the first is the picture of a static society — that Britain was essentially the same in the first as it was in the fourth century AD. The second is one of geographical uniformity — that the 'Romans' were the same everywhere in Britain. The third is that in AD 410 the glories of Roman Britain were suddenly extinguished and Britain was plunged instantly into the barbarities of the 'dark ages'. There is a grain of truth in each notion; but this chapter sketches the evolving shape of Roman Britain and colours in some of the contrasts.

The conquest

Julius Caesar's adventures in 55 and 54 BC did not constitute a conquest; he merely (as the historian Tacitus observed) 'pointed out' Britain to his successors; and he left no visible traces.

Nearly a century later, in AD 43, four legions with auxiliary support landed at Richborough and pressed on, with heavy fighting on the Medway, towards the British capital of Colchester. Here they were joined by their commander-in-chief, the Emperor Claudius, who supervised the capture of Colchester and received the surrender of much, but not all, of Britain. The following season the army divided to advance south-westwards, north-westwards and north and to establish a provisional frontier obliquely across the island (roughly from Exeter to the Humber). South of this was the first *province*, studded with temporary or semi-permanent garrisons (such as Hod Hill, Dorset, 6) and governed first from Colchester but very soon from London. This was the Lowland Zone, the richest and most developed part of Britain, and the agricultural and mineral resources were rapidly harnessed to the new economic structure. The British farmer paid taxes in kind and in the new coinage, supporting a now distant occupying army of some forty thousand men and supplying a fast growing urban population in the new towns and cities. Pressures on the rural communities were severe, and the response in the late first and early second centuries was the 'first wave' of *villas*, managed largely by prosperous Britons but occasionally, as the opportunities for investment were realised, owned by overseas entrepreneurs. Roughly half of Britain was soon united, politically by the new bureaucracy and physically by a superb system of roads and inland waterways. Rapid Romanisation, however, and even wilful mismanagement of the province brought the inevitable backlash in about AD 60; certain kings, notably Cogidubnus in Sussex and Prasutagus in East Anglia, had been allowed to retain their kingdoms for their lifetimes; in the latter case, a misunderstanding over the succession precipitated a revolt that brought to a head the long-standing grievances of the Britons. Led by the rejected queen, Boudicca, the rebels devastated Colchester, St Albans and London in a matter of weeks and were equally swiftly and ruthlessly suppressed by the army that entered the province once more from its frontier posts. The province took some years to recover from this blow to its precarious stability.

Beyond the frontier, moreover, British resistance was hardening, and a dynastic dispute in northern *Brigantia* provided the opportunity between AD 71 and 74 to crush a large concentration of organised British opposition and to annex a large portion of northern territory. The piecemeal acquisition of the rest of Britain is like the completion of a jigsaw. Wales proved the hardest task; operating from Wroxeter (Shropshire, 1), the army had barely subdued North Wales and Anglesey when it was recalled to confront Boudicca's hordes. The Silures of South Wales had defied Rome since the 40s and it was not until AD 78 that the task was more or less completed. The price for Rome was the death, through sheer exhaustion, of a fine governor and the creation of expensive legionary fortresses at Caerleon (Gwent, 2) in the south and at Chester (Cheshire, 1) in the north. With a further fortress at Lincoln, the enlarged province was now secure for a century or more. The final piece of the jigsaw, the vast and unprofitable tracts of *Caledonia*, was acquired through the energetic efforts of the most celebrated governor, Agricola (78-84); in five campaigning seasons he filled northern Britain with camps and forts whose 'Agricolan origins' will be frequently noted later in this book. Although British resistance was now effectively broken, this distant territory was never Romanised and the northern frontier was withdrawn by Trajan and his successor, Hadrian, to the line that was finally secured by the great wall.

The northern frontier

Hadrian's Wall was begun in 122 and completed after many modifications (pages 60-76). For a decade and a half it effectively 'separated the Romans from the barbarians', as a contemporary put it. By 139, however, an advance into Lowland Scotland was once more deemed necessary, and under the Emperor Antoninus Pius a more northerly frontier line was adopted — the Antonine Wall (pages 174-7). With a short break in about 158, this frontier held the turbulent northerners at bay, until a final crisis in 163 caused the abandonment of Scotland and the recommissioning of Hadrian's Wall. This line, too, was breached in 197 when the Governor, Clodius Albinus, removed most of the garrison of Britain in an unsuccessful bid for the purple. Energetic campaigning by a new Governor and subsequently, from 208-11, by the Emperor Severus in person amounted to a 'reconquest' of much of Britain; the hand of Severus can still be detected in many sites, military and civilian, described below; and he was the first Emperor to die in Britain (at York, in 211).

The years of peace (c 213-342)

The third century in Britain is best seen as a period of consolidation — and of relative security in comparison with the continent. There was little new building in towns and villas, mainly repair and maintenance. Many towns had responded to the troubles at the end of the previous century by erecting earthen defences; within the next 150 years most of these, with some fresh communities, could afford walls. Steady prosperity in the countryside is seen in several new mosaics. But the coasts were increasingly vulnerable to raiding parties from northern France and the Low Countries — the ancestors of the Saxons; and the beginnings of the chain of coastal forts — the 'Saxon Shore' — belong to this period. In 286 the commander of the Channel Fleet, Carausius, had been so successful in suppressing the pirates (or, as some said, in coming to terms with them) that he was emboldened to declare himself emperor of a separatist empire of Britain and the nearer part of Gaul. This episode lasted a mere ten years, but it showed how easily the more distant provinces could be lost.

The Albinus affair of 197 had already prompted the division of Britain into two provinces, *Superior* (i.e. nearer to Rome) and *Inferior* (with York as its capital). In 284 Diocletian's reorganisation of the entire Empire took this further, by dividing Britain into *four* provinces (whose boundaries are uncertain); these four (to which a fifth was added in 369) formed the *Diocese* of the Britains, which in turn joined other dioceses to form the *Prefecture* of the Gauls, the whole being one part of the Western Empire. Both East and West were united for a space under Constantine the Great (306-37). His edict of 313, the Edict of Milan, made Christianity legal, and the following year the British church sent three bishops to the Council of Arles. The early fourth century is marked by the 'second wave' of villas, either new (in the north) or extensively rebuilt (in the south); for the large estates were best equipped to survive a period of rampant inflation and social hardship that forced many small farmers or peasants into debt-bondage and even vagrancy. Superficially, however, all seemed well; and the solid material remains that we see today are generally those of the fourth century. Moreover, Britain still looked safe to foreign investors.

The last years

Sporadic trouble on the northern frontier for more than half a century came to a head in 367 in the 'Barbarian Conspiracy', when the Picts (of Scotland), the Scots (of Ireland), the Saxons and others combined to overwhelm Britain. Hadrian's Wall was overrun, the Count of the Saxon Shore was killed and the Duke of the Britains cut off. A new commander, Theodosius, was sent to Britain with a strong field army; in two years' hard fighting Britain was rescued once again.

How far the towns and villas of Lowland Britain suffered at this time is archaeologically uncertain. The Theodosian reconstruction, however, is not only visible on many sites but was clearly effective, to judge from the continued prosperity of villas and towns until at least the end of the fourth century. Lawlessness in the countryside was increasing, however; by the end of the century harvested corn was brought for drying into the towns or even the villa houses, as at Brading (Isle of Wight, 1). The towns themselves were fortified strongpoints, often with bastions added to the walls and wider, flat-bottomed ditches. Urban communities strengthened their self-defence with the employment of mercenary garrisons of Germanic soldiers — the 'prior Saxonisation' that paved the way for full Saxon settlement after the link with Rome was finally broken in 410. Coastal defence was strengthened with the building of signal stations on the Yorkshire coast in the 370s, while frontier posts were manned by a kind of peasant militia. By 407 the entire regular army had been withdrawn on various pretexts and in 410 the youthful Emperor Honorius instructed the British cities to look to their own defence.

The military and bureaucratic ties with Rome were broken; but life in the villages, the estates and the towns had to continue. There is evidence both for large-scale but sporadic emigration to the continent and for the peaceful assimilation of new immigrants. As late as 446 the British cities sent a last appeal to Rome (the 'Groans of the Britons'); but the cry went unheard. The Empire was dying, and Roman Britain had now become part of Europe.

A SIMPLIFIED LIST OF ROMAN EMPERORS

31 BC- AD 14	AUGUSTUS)
14-37	TIBERIUS)
37-41	GAIUS) *Julio-* (Caligula)) *Claudians*
41-54	CLAUDIUS)
54-68	NERO)
68-69	Galba, Otho, Vitellius (*Year of the Four* *Emperors*)
69-79	VESPASIAN)
79-81	TITUS) *Flavians*
81-96	DOMITIAN)
96-98	NERVA *
98-117	TRAJAN *
117-138	HADRIAN *
136-161	ANTONINUS) PIUS *)*Antonines*
161-180	MARCUS) AURELIUS *)
180-192	COMMODUS
193-197	Pertinax, Gaius Pescennius Niger, Severus Julianus, and Clodius Albinus
197-211	SEPTIMUS SEVERUS
211-217	CARACALLA
211-212	(Geta)
217-218	MACRINUS
218-222	ELEGABALUS
222-235	SEVERUS ALEXANDER
235-238	MAXIMINUS I etc
238-244	GORDIANUS III
244-249	PHILIPPUS
249-251	TRAJAN DECIUS
251-253	TREBONIANUS GALLUS
253-259	VALERIANUS
259-268	GALLIENUS etc (including Tetricus I and II in Gaul)

268-270	CLAUDIUS II (Gothicus etc)
270-275	AURELIANUS etc
275-276	TACITUS
276-281	PROBUS
281-283	CARUS
286-296	CARAUSIUS and ALLECTUS
284-305	DIOCLETIAN (E) MAXIMIANUS (W)
305-306	GALERIUS (E) CONSTANTIUS (W)
306-324	CONSTANTINE I (the Great) Maxentius, Licinius
324-337	CONSTANTINE THE GREAT
337-361	Constantine's sons
361-363	JULIAN THE APOSTATE
363-364	JOVIANUS
364-375	VALENTINIANUS (W) VALENS (E)
367	GRATIAN co-emperor
375-383	GRATIAN (W) and VALENTINIAN (W 378) THEODOSIUS (E)
383-388	MAXIMIUS (W)
395-408	ARCADIUS (E)
395-423	HONORIUS (W)
425-475	seven minor figures (W)
408-527	successors of Arcadius (E)
475-476	ROMULUS AUGUSTULUS (W) *Deposed, traditional end* *of Roman Empire in the* *West.*
527-565	JUSTINIAN (E)

* the 'five good emperors'

3. The countryside

Native settlements

With a few rare examples (not now visitable) there are no rural settlements of distinctively Roman type. The countryside, especially in the Highland Zone, remained relatively uninfluenced by Rome. For a three-dimensional impression of the native settlement type a visit to Butser (Hampshire) is recommended, to be followed perhaps by visits to Wessex settlements such as Woodcuts (Dorset, 11) and Rotherley (Wiltshire, 2). Material changes included the adoption of Roman coinage and pottery, and even painted wall plaster, and the traditional round-houses sometimes gave way to rectangular houses with stone walls and thatched or even tiled roofs. Settlements in Cornwall, Wales and north Britain remained almost defiantly Celtic.

The roads and forts, however, influenced the siting of new, open settlements — the *vici*. Some developed into small market towns at crossroads and at the sites of forts when the army moved on. Rural industries played their part, too, as at the mining settlement of Charterhouse-on-Mendip (Somerset, 1).

In many cases the configuration of the immediate landscape has survived, and the sub-rectangular 'Celtic fields' and terraced strip lynchets can be made out. These are mentioned when they are clearly visible, preferably by evening light when the shadows emphasise the relief, or in autumn and winter when the vegetation is low.

Roads

These are among the most numerous surviving remains of the Roman period and the most rewarding for the persistent field worker. A few of the best are described (see Index), but most of the others can be traced with the aid of the Ordnance Survey maps at 1:50,000. Their legendary straightness was frequently modified to suit the terrain, and a 'flexible line of straight pieces' is a better description. Construction varied considerably. The norm was a 3.7 to 4.5 metres wide strip of rammed gravel or local equivalent (such as iron slag) on a coarser foundation and often renewed. The road was invariably accompanied by side ditches, often at some distance, for drainage and to demarcate a 'road zone' that had to be kept clear of vegetation and potential dangers. Travellers were exempt from the law that forbade the carrying of weapons in public. The most prominent feature is often an embankment, or *agger*, even where it appears structurally unnecessary and was presumably built to impress. Bridges were generally of wood; milestones were rare and generally unhelpful for route finding; changes of horses and hot baths were sometimes available at road stations (*mansiones*), especially for those travelling on official business or engaged in the *cursus publicus* or state post. For these, see the Index.

Villas

A simple cottage or farmhouse can constitute a 'villa', but the term should properly include the land as well. Such houses seldom merit preservation today, but frequently they are to be found embedded in something more complex. The evolution of many villa plans is fascinating and by no means standard. Most were of the 'corridor type', the corridor or verandah connecting rooms in series. The 'winged corridor type' was frequently a modification of this, the wings either projecting forwards or forming an H in plan. The most elaborate plan is the 'courtyard villa', in which ranges of rooms or separate buildings were grouped around one or more courtyards; sometimes they enclosed a walled farmyard, sometimes a garden. A common form of outbuilding was the large aisled barn, generally much modified by long use; the well and the corn drier were both Roman innovations, the latter resembling a small hypocaust.

In the house the principal room, generally centrally placed, was the reception room or dining room, usually with mosaic floor and painted walls. Dining areas were often semicircular, reflecting the classical three-couch arrangement. Other rooms, such as bedrooms, are hard to identify, though narrow spaces on plan are often thought to denote staircases to upper storeys. Kitchens generally prove disappointingly primitive to the twentieth-century visitor. Bath suites were miniature versions of the large urban establishments, often in a separate wing for safety reasons. The *hypocausts* for under-floor heating are usually prominent, with their brick pillars supporting thick floors of concrete and often mosaic. Contrast the heating channels under the floors of living rooms, where the masses of masonry between the radiating channels acted as storage heaters for prolonged, gentle heat; the pillared variety could be heated rapidly, as required.

4. The towns

The pre-Roman pattern of *tribes* was adopted by the Romans for their *civitates* or administrative regions. The *civitas capitals* were therefore new Roman towns either on the site of pre-Roman settlements or on fresh sites when the focus of power had to be moved from a hillfort. The pre-Roman aristocracy, who presumably owned the new villa estates around the towns, provided the magistrates and town council, all by election. The community was therefore to a large extent self-governing. Of higher status was the *municipium*, whose constitution was governed by a charter and whose citizens had a limited form of Roman citizenship. Of at least half a dozen possible examples in Britain, *Verulamium* (St Albans) is the only fairly certain case. Only four cities in Britain are known to have enjoyed the highest rank, that of *colonia*. Three — Colchester, Gloucester and Lincoln — were early foundations, true to the principle that a large proportion of the citizens were retired veterans — a spearhead of Romanisation, in effect, and a bastion against rebellion. The fourth, York, received its charter as late as the early third century, while London (renamed *Augusta*) is a further possibility. The constitution of a *colonia* was modelled on that of Rome, and its burghers were Roman citizens (all provincials, however, became citizens by imperial decree in 212).

Most Romano-British towns and cities were permitted to erect *fortifications* — more, we suspect, from civic pride than from military necessity at the time. There are a few first-century examples, but there seems to have been a spate of earthen defences at the end of the second century. These could be thrown up relatively cheaply and rapidly; some towns, but by no means all, achieved the next stage, the addition of a wall, at various times in the next two centuries. In the troubled years of the later fourth century true military necessity prompted the addition of bastions for artillery and new ditches. In this we might see the influence of the Saxon Shore forts and the superb defences of some continental towns. Gateways, on the other hand, had always been strong, with towered guardhouses. The implications, in terms of predicting population size and estimating cost and manpower for defence, are important; and it is worth noting the rethinking at Silchester (Hampshire, 8).

Town-houses can often be seen in Britain, in both 'parades' of shops and *insulae*, or blocks (at St Albans, Hertfordshire, 2), or — like small villas — in their own grounds (at Dorchester, Dorset, 5). They, like the villas, were often adorned with mosaics, hypocausts and painted wall plaster; of the last, a noteworthy example is the

Painted House at Dover, outside the walls of the earlier fort (Kent, 3). This reminds us of the open settlements, or *vici*, that grew up outside military installations and which can be seen, for example, at *Vindolanda* and Housesteads (Hadrian's Wall, 12 and 13). In contrast to the villas, bath suites are normally lacking, as the urban *public baths* satisfied this everyday need.

Public baths, most magnificently seen at Wroxeter (Shropshire, 1) and Leicester, were one of the amenities provided by the city fathers or by private munificence. Their preserved remains often seem complex but are the elaboration of a simple sequence. The bather first undressed in the *apodyterium*, passed through the cold *frigidarium* to the warmer *tepidarium* and the hot *caldarium*, which was next to the furnace and contained a hot bath. The steam opened the pores of the skin and induced sweating; the dirt was removed not with soap but with oil and a curved *strigil* or scraper. Massage could be part of the process, which continued with a leisurely return through the rooms in reverse order to the *frigidarium*, to end with a sharp cold plunge and a rub down with a towel. Plunge baths were for wallowing in, not swimming, and the adjoining *palaestra* was a court for physical exercise. At the great curative establishment at Bath (Avon, 1), the military bath-house at Chesters (Hadrian's Wall, 8) and elsewhere can be seen an alternative system — the Spartan room or *laconicum*. This involved sweating in dry heat.

Another popular recreation was the shows in the *amphitheatre*, which was strictly elliptical in plan by contrast with the semi-circular *theatre*. The amphitheatre (which was normally outside the walls) was the venue for gladiatorial combats and animal sports, with martial displays in the military towns. Theatres were less common, presumably used for more decorous entertainments (often perhaps of a religious nature) and public meetings.

The *forum* was the civic centre and market place, centrally placed at the intersection of the principal streets of the grid plan. At one side was the *basilica*, the largest covered meeting hall, used for the dispensation of justice and administration (e.g. when the governor, his judges and officials were on circuit). Official hospitality was provided in the *mansio* — a term used not only for civic inns but also for the road stations, such as Wall (Staffordshire, 1). Other public buildings would include *temples* (see chapter 5), monumental *arches* and public *fountains*. These two categories are not, on the whole, preserved in Britain, though the observant visitor will note the almost obsessive care taken over both *sewerage* and the water supply. The latter was achieved through the *aqueduct*, seldom arched and normally an open leat or stream. That for Dorchester can still be traced (Dorset, 5), and the masonry of a military example is visible at Corbridge (Hadrian's Wall, 5, illustration 23).

5. Religious monuments

The state religion of Rome was imposed upon the Britons in the form of temples of classical style, each served by a college of priests maintained at public expense. In contrast to the Greek form, the Roman temple was set on a high platform (*podium*), to be seen from the front and approached by a flight of steps. Freestanding columns supported a triangular pediment forming a porch, beyond which stood the *cella*, or shrine that contained the cult statue. Such temples were not common in Britain, but those of Bath and Colchester are noteworthy.

Temples in the ancient world were not congregational, and worship took place in the open air around an altar in front. This was so for the commonest type, the Romano-Celtic temple; here the *cella* formed a squat tower, with an ambulatory or verandah around it — the ground plan comprising two concentric squares. Circular and polygonal variants are known, and sometimes a solid outer wall replaced the pillared ambulatory. Celtic deities were numerous and usually of purely local importance; dedications to them, and their powerful sculptured heads, should be noted in many museums.

Oriental temples, dedicated to the Persian Mithras, Egyptian Isis and so on, are known. In form they are frequently apsed, with

2. A typical Romano-Celtic temple.

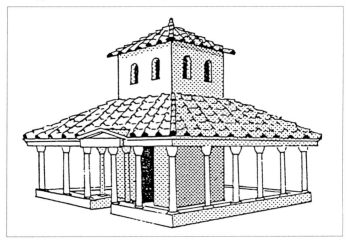

a nave and aisles, designed for small congregations. They resemble Christian churches, of which a few have been identified, though only one (Colchester, Essex 3, illustration 13) can be visited today. We have yet to find a synagogue in Roman Britain.

Tombstones, often with sculptured reliefs, are to be found in most major museums, and their inscriptions can be very revealing: urban examples speak of child mortality and short adult lives, prosperous British tradesmen and immigrants from distant provinces. Soldiers' careers, on the other hand, are invaluable to military historians. Cemeteries were invariably outside town walls (a legal requirement), beside the main roads to catch the attention of passers by. A few large tombs and mausolea have survived and can be visited.

6. Military remains

By the first century AD the Roman army was composed of distinct units of *legions* and *auxilia*. The legions were the backbone of the army, 'Roman' in that their members were full citizens of Italian or (as time went on) provincial origins, excellently disciplined, trained and equipped. The full strength of a legion was about 5,200 men organised into ten cohorts, each divided into six centuries of eighty men commanded by centurions. The first cohort was larger, consisting of five double centuries. In battle, the legions were expected to take on the heaviest fighting, and in peacetime to carry out every kind of engineering project — particularly in the earlier years of the occupation when civilian architects and contractors hardly existed. Service was normally for 25 years, with good, regular pay and a gratuity on discharge as a veteran. The auxiliaries were less regular native troops from all parts of the known world, often bringing special skills such as horsemanship, archery and tracking. Their organisation and equipment resembled that of the legions, but individual units retained much of their native character and language. Until Roman citizenship was made universal they were guaranteed citizenship (and an inscribed bronze *diploma* as proof) on discharge.

Britons were attracted into the army as auxiliaries, to be posted abroad, and even (with the passing of time) recruited as legionaries. The principle of never employing auxiliaries in their country of origin was soon relaxed, and there were Britons in Agricola's army campaigning in *Caledonia*. Stationed for much of their lives in garrison forts, both legionaries and auxiliaries kept (unofficial) wives and families in the *vici* or extramural civil settlements and themselves settled there on discharge. Sons followed in fathers' footsteps, and so by the end of the period the army in Britain was essentially Celtic, and indeed largely British — an important point that is not generally appreciated.

By 410, when the last pay chests had arrived from Rome, the troops must have accepted that they were Britons defending their homeland as a native British army. The structure of the army had changed fundamentally with the reorganisations of Diocletian and Constantine; the distinction was no longer between legionaries and auxiliaries, but between static frontier forces (*limitanei*) and mobile field armies (*comitatenses*) commanded by, for instance, the Duke of the Britains and the Count of the Saxon Shore. The *limitanei* were the inferior force, with what was left of the old legionary structure (we know this from the *Notitia Dignitatum*, a fourth-century list of units and official posts); barbarians who penetrated the frontiers and trouble that arose within the provinces would be dealt with by the *comitatenses*. An important change was the new practice of quartering these mobile strike forces in the fortified towns. Of the living conditions in the frontier posts we still know relatively little, though excavations at Portchester (Hampshire, 5) and the newly conserved 'chalets' replacing the barracks at Housesteads (Hadrian's Wall, 12) give some idea of physical change.

The fleet was an arm of the army, with an important role in transport and liaison at the conquest and in subsequent campaigns. It was known, until the second century, as the *Classis Britannica* (the tile stamp *CL BR* is often met); it was a much changed fleet that patrolled the English Channel under Carausius and later, or scoured the Bristol Channel and the Yorkshire coast to intercept raiders and warn the signal stations.

Of the permanent army bases, the legionary fortresses are the most spectacular, distinguished by massive masonry defences and interval towers like city walls, and with stone buildings inside. At 20 hectares they are larger versions of the forts that housed the auxiliary units. These last, like the earlier phases of the legionary fortresses, originally had ramparts of earth or clay with timber breastworks, towered gates and rounded corners, fronted by one or more V-shaped ditches. Sizes generally range from 1 to 3 hectares, often more. A reconstructed example, peculiar in plan but orthodox in structure, is the Lunt, Baginton (Warwickshire, 1). Permanency in such defences was later ensured by the addition of a stone facing to the rampart and the general use of masonry for internal buildings. The quadrilateral plan (with four principal entrances) is reflected in the grid of internal roads and the arrangement of barrack blocks, cavalry stables, granaries, workshops and individual buildings such as the

3. The tile stamp of the Classis Britannica, or British fleet.

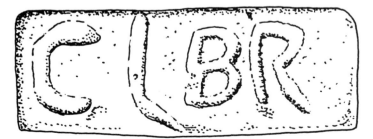

hospital (*valetudinarium*). In the centre stood the headquarters (*principia*), with courtyard enclosed by offices and stores (with verandahs for shelter while queuing), strongroom, shrine for the standards and a large cross-hall like the *basilica* of a town. Next to the *principia* is usually the *praetorium*, or commandant's house and officers' mess, where a private bath suite is an occasional luxury. The bath-house for the fort is always found outside it; this, with the shops, inns and brothels of the *vicus* that grew up around the walls, provided the soldier's off-duty recreation.

This basic layout is the same for the semi-permanent fort and the marching camp. It was normal practice on campaign to make camp each night — an earthen rampart crowned with a timber palisade (prepared stakes for which were carried by the men), often irregular in shape on uneven ground and ditched when possible. Tents held six men each, with larger and more individual ones for centurions, officers, *principia* and *praetorium*. Entrances were defended in two ways: either by a *titulum*, a short bank and ditch across and outside the gap in the rampart, or by a *clavicula*, a curved continuation of the rampart inside the camp. The latter tends to be the earlier form, generally obsolete by the second century. It is interesting to see the care taken over corners and entrances in the most ephemeral type of earthwork, the practice camps. These are often indistinguishable from the semi-permanent camps but those that are clearly non-functional are listed as practice camps in the Index.

The fortlets are the smallest category of permanent post, square with banks, ditches and occasionally stone walls; the milecastles of Hadrian's Wall are a specialised form of fortlet. So, too, are the signal stations of the Welsh and Yorkshire coasts in the later fourth century. The idea of the watchtower with earthworks at its feet is an earlier idea, found on the Gask frontier, the Rhine frontier (as depicted on Trajan's Column) and — again in specialised form — as the interval turret on Hadrian's Wall.

7. Roman sites in England

1. Bath *Aquae Sulis* ST 751647

The natural hot springs attracted Roman settlement from the mid or late first century and the town soon developed as a spa, with the waters dedicated to Sulis-Minerva, a blending of native and Roman deities. In the late third or early fourth century the town was defended by a wall enclosing 9.3 hectares; the course of this wall may be approximately followed, at least on the north, west and south sides, by the medieval wall indicated by Upper and Lower Borough Walls, Sawclose and Westgate. Despite the walls, the character of this spa town is far from clear. No forum, for instance, has been discovered. A theatre is suspected beneath the Abbey, and a smaller bath-house (not visitable) is known in addition to the principal baths complex. By the end of the fourth century the baths had become disused and silted up by floods. In the eighth century its remains were described in the Saxon poem *The Ruin*.

Of the public buildings so far discovered the chief are the baths, a large part of which is open to the public for an admission fee. They underwent several changes during the Roman period. The focal point of the baths is the Sacred Spring, with its surrounding reservoir, from which the waters emerge at 46.5^{0}C, limited by a polygonal enclosure and lined with sheeting of Mendip lead. Into this spring votive offerings were cast in Roman times, and those since recovered are displayed in the Roman Baths Museum. To the south is the complex system of baths, of which the chief are the Circular Bath, the Great Bath and the Eastern Baths. The Great Bath, which still retains its original lining of lead sheeting (doubtless from Mendip), was for swimming.

North-west of the reservoir was the Temple of Sulis-Minerva. It is no longer exposed, but objects derived from it, including the pediment with the head of Medusa, the bronze head of Minerva and many sculptured and inscribed funerary and other slabs, are in the Roman Baths Museum north of the Great Bath. A replica of the portico of this temple, reflecting the archaeological knowledge of 1909 when it was built, is in Sydney Gardens behind the Holburne of Menstrie Museum. East of this temple was an altar with four carved corners, one of which is now built into the north-east corner of Compton Dando church (ST 645646), and two of the others are back *in situ* in the temple precinct in the museum. The labyrinthine underground tour is a remarkable experience, at last enabling the visitor (although still with difficulty) to under-

4. *Bath, Avon: the Roman bath, with its eighteenth-century superstructure.*

5. *Bath, Avon: the Gorgon pediment of the temple.*

stand the relationship of the various parts of the complex.

A mosaic floor, probably of a town house, may be seen in the basement of the Royal Mineral Water Hospital within Upper Borough Walls, by enquiring at the entrance.

In the surrounding countryside are the sites of numerous villas. A network of roads, including the Fosse Way, connected Bath with Sea Mills, Cirencester, Silchester, Ilchester and elsewhere.

2. Keynsham: villa and building

ST 645692 (villa);
ST 656689 (building)

The A4175 runs on an embankment across the villa, most of which lay in the town cemetery; the building is at the entrance to the grounds of Cadbury's (formerly Fry's) factory, Somerdale.

The sumptuous courtyard villa dates from the late third century. Of some thirty rooms, seventeen were uncovered in 1922-4 and were destroyed to make room for further burials in the cemetery. There were at least ten mosaics. Those from a room south of the road included scenes of Europa and the Bull, Minerva playing a double pipe, and birds with branches and fruit. A small part of the north corridor, comprising some steps, may be seen in the cemetery between the mortuary chapel and the road.

The small square building was a separate discovery in 1922 when the factory was being built. To avoid resiting the factory its foundations were rebuilt near the entrance to the factory site. Proposed redevelopment makes the future of the reconstruction uncertain at the time of writing (1993). The mosaics, formerly on view in the site museum and in the factory, are now safely stored in Keynsham but inaccessible. Their long-term future, too, is under review.

3. Kings Weston: villa

ST 534776

On the south side of Long Cross, near its west end. Key obtainable from Blaise Castle House Museum, Henbury, Bristol (telephone: 0272 506789).

There were two buildings, of which the eastern was excavated in 1948-50. It was built between *c.* 270 and 300 and was altered and added to at various times before being abandoned towards the end of the fourth century, possibly in 367-8. The west wing (rooms II to VII), covered by a modern wooden building for protection, includes most of a bath suite and a room (VI) now used as a site museum for the study of rural life in Roman Britain. This room is floored partly with a mosaic from a villa at Brislington (Bristol). Room VII has a geometrical mosaic. Many finds are in Bristol City Museum.

4. Sea Mills *Abonae*: settlement   ST 551759

The site is beside the A4 and opposite Sea Mills railway station.

The site, at the confluence of the Bristol Avon with the river Trym, probably started as a small fort in the first century and later became a ferry terminal on the route between Caerleon and Silchester and a trading centre. The only visible remains are the foundations of a building at the junction of Roman Way and the Portway. An inscribed Roman tombstone from Old Sneed Park to the south-east is in Bristol City Museum, which houses many other finds from Sea Mills.

BERKSHIRE

1. Knighton Bushes: settlement   SU 300830

Approached by a minor road from Upper Lambourn, then by a cart track.

On the hillside to the west of Knighton Bushes are the remains of approximately 800 hectares of 'Celtic fields', together with at least three Romano-British settlements and a cross-dyke. These cover a wide area, stretching almost as far north as the Ridgeway and to Ashdown Park on the west. Little is to be seen of these settlements. One is sub-rectangular and encloses about 0.4 hectares. It lies due west of Knighton Bushes Plantation at SU 298831. A second rectangular settlement lies between Woolstone Down and Uffington Down. It is on the north edge of the fields (SU 302853) but is separated from them by a massive cross-ridge dyke. The third settlement is roughly polygonal and encloses about 0.8 hectares. It lies east of the small wood at Compton Bottom (SU 286843) and trial excavation produced Romano-British occupation material.

Ancient tracks through the Celtic fields lead from the settlements and join south of the Knighton Bushes Plantation site.

2. Lowbury Hill: building   SU 540823

3 km north-east of Compton along a bridle road.

A rectangular earthwork enclosure covers the flint footings of walls, with an entrance in the middle of the eastern side. Excavations showed that two corners contained timber buildings with tiled roofs; in the south-west corner at the base of the wall was the burial of a middle-aged woman with a cleft skull. This was interpreted as a dedication. The site was apparently occupied in the iron age and the walled enclosure was in use from *c.*200 to *c.* 400. The site has been variously interpreted as a farm and a Romano-Celtic temple.

A pagan Saxon burial was found in the barrow outside the farm entrance. It was a primary burial.

25

BUCKINGHAMSHIRE

1. Bancroft, Milton Keynes: villa   SP 827403

The villa lies north-west of Milton Keynes, in Millers Way, Bradwell. Approach via the A422 from the A5, and turn left at the second roundabout. The site is part of the city parks network; there is a car park and access is not restricted.

Initially threatened by development, the main house and six farm buildings (three rectangular, three circular) were excavated in 1973-8 and 1983-5. Upon an iron age settlement, the first stone and timber building of *c.*AD 100 with a small bath suite and outbuildings was replaced, after a fire *c.*170, by a winged corridor house in stone. In *c.*340 the baths were rebuilt and the house was extended, with mosaics, a walled garden, central fishpond and octagonal summerhouse. In the twelfth century the ruins were apparently robbed for the building of Bradwell Abbey. The cemetery, in use from the first century onwards, lay 300 metres to the north-west; a square mausoleum, with two burials, was built in the fourth century and demolished *c.*400 though burials continued. A small early Saxon timber building was found nearby.

The mausoleum is not now visible, but the villa site has been marked out with explanatory signs and the fishpond reconstructed.

2. Thornborough Mounds: barrows   SP 732333

Clearly visible on the north side of the A421, 230 metres east of Thornborough Bridge.

Both of these large Roman barrows were opened by the Duke of Buckingham in about 1840. One was presumed to have been opened previously; the other contained fragments of pottery and glass, a gold ornament and a ring, two bronze jugs, a two-handled bowl and lamp, two wine jars and traces of iron weapons scattered on a rough limestone floor. The corpse seems to have been cremated on this floor and then covered over by some kind of timber structure. The burial was probably of second-century date. Both barrows are well preserved, that on the east standing 4 metres high and 27 metres in diameter, the western one being 4.9 metres high and 37 metres in diameter.

The barrows are sited close to the junction of five Roman roads. 110 metres south of the river bridge, in a field on the western bank of the stream, a small square Romano-Celtic temple was excavated in 1964. It had contained a central sanctuary 5.2 metres square, surrounded by a verandah, with a porch and entrance facing eastwards to the river and barrows. It was erected about 265 and destroyed between 410 and 420. Nothing remains to be seen today.

CAMBRIDGESHIRE

1. Car Dyke: canal   TL 465702 to TL 496643

A series of canals (not all certainly navigable) was cut to help drain the Fens and to carry grain and other produce to troops in Lincolnshire and York (see also Lincolnshire, 3). The first section links the river Cam at Waterbeach with the Old West River 3 km south-east of Aldreth, a distance of about 8 km. Excavations in 1947 showed that the Car Dyke was very similar in dimensions to modern barge canals, being 13.7 metres wide and 2.1 metres deep at surface level, with a flat bottom 8.5 metres wide. A number of Romano-British settlements have been discovered close to the dyke. One of these is at TL 465702. It consists of low banks and shallow depressions and may be reached along farm roads off the B1049 leading to Setchel Fen. The site is not very impressive. The Car Dyke consists for the most part of a wet ditch and lies beside the main Cambridge to Ely road (A10) as it passes Waterbeach airfield at TL 485664.

2. Castor: town   TL 125985

The site of the Roman town is in the modern village, on Stocks Hill, opposite the church.

A modern wall across from the church has two chunks of Roman masonry projecting from it. These are the last visible remains *in situ* of a substantial building in a large settlement or small town that was connected with the pottery industry operating in the valley of the river Nene, and which gave its name to the Castor ware to be seen in most museums (see also Water Newton, Cambridgeshire, 6).

The prosperity of the owners of these potteries is clear from the mosaics recorded in the nineteenth century from the town and at least one villa in the region. One of these, a simple geometric design, can be seen today relaid in the old dairy at Milton Hall.

3. Chesterton: barrow   TL 129946

A probable Roman barrow on top of the hill 800 metres west of the A1 and 800 metres south of Chesterton. Nothing is known of its contents.

4. Great Stukeley: barrow   TL 219748

A probable Roman barrow on the north side of the A14, the Ermine Street Roman road.

5. Orton Longueville: camp and villa   TL 149977

Turn off the A605 3 km east of the junction with the A1 near Water Newton and 5 km west of Peterborough. Follow the signs to Nene

Park Ferry Meadows.

This site was excavated in 1972-4 and the Roman buildings are now marked out in the recreation grounds, near the information centre and the car park. The corner is visible of a military ditch of the first century, part of two temporary camps with multiple ditches. Immediately across the river at Longthorpe was an 11 hectares legionary and auxiliary base, now invisible in the golf course.

The main villa buildings have not been excavated, but an aisled building, probably of the third century, is now marked out on the site, with a well and a small building that might have been a temple. This was of the concentric variety, with a central square timber *cella* on stone footings and a surrounding timber verandah. Other features, including a corn drier and a possible fishpond, are not now visible.

6. Water Newton *Durobrivae*: town   TL 122968

There is a lay-by on the A1 adjoining this site.

East of the modern village lies the Roman town of *Durobrivae*. It is situated in a triangle between the modern road (A1), the river Nene and a stream called the Billing Brook. It grew up at the point where Ermine Street crossed the Nene and was the centre of the largest industrial complex so far known from Roman Britain, manufacturing pottery on a grand scale. It is about 18 hectares in extent and defended by a wall, rampart and ditch, but little is to be seen on the ground today save for the earthworks surrounding the site and the *agger* of the Ermine Street branching north-west-wards from the bend in the A1. A bypass ran outside the walls on the eastern side. Aerial photographs have revealed a Roman fort in the field between *Durobrivae* and Water Newton village; nothing can be seen of it on the ground.

In 1874 and again in 1975 hoards of treasure were found at Water Newton, which are now in the British Museum. The treasure includes the earliest known group of Christian silver from anywhere in the Roman Empire. Nine vessels and nineteen plaques were found, as well as a gold disc and thirty gold coins of the fourth century AD. Unfortunately the objects were not found under excavation conditions.

CHESHIRE

1. Chester *Deva*: fortress   SJ 405665 (centre)

The site of the present city was chosen for the building of a legionary fortress, which with others at York (North Yorkshire, 8) and Caerleon (Gwent, 2) formed the basis for the defence of Britain. The fortress was constructed between AD 76 and 80,

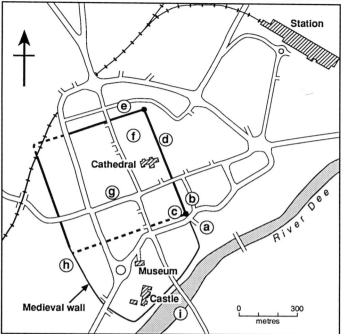

6. *Plan of Chester showing the sites described in the text: a, Newgate amphitheatre; b, fortress wall; c, 'Roman Gardens'; d, Kaleyards; e, North Wall; f, Abbey Green; g, Goss Street; h, Roodee; i, Handbridge.*

although a small fort may have existed there as early as 60. The site had the advantage of easy supply by sea and stood at the lowest practicable crossing of the river Dee.

The first legionary fortress had timber buildings and an earthen rampart with a timber palisade and surrounding ditch, and it enclosed almost 25 hectares. During the second century the defences were rebuilt in stone from quarries on the south side of the Dee; the surviving portions of the fortress belong to this period. The later history of the site is not clear, but it almost certainly formed a strategic link in the defence of the west coast against piratical raids from Ireland. Inscriptions show that the XX Legion provided the garrison during most of the Roman occupation, but the II Legion was also stationed there initially for a short time.

Within the limits of the fortress, excavations have revealed the remains of the *principia*, barrack buildings, granaries, ovens, numerous hypocausts, towers and rampart buildings. Extramural

29

structures include an amphitheatre and the remains of a quay wall. The main cemetery was outside the fortress on the north-west side.

The Grosvenor Museum contains much material from excavations in the city, including numerous inscribed and sculptured stones mostly found in the north wall between 1883 and 1892.

The best visible remains in the city are:

a. Newgate: amphitheatre. The southern half was under the grounds of the former Ursuline convent. The northern half was excavated and opened to the public in 1972. Replacing a timber structure (not now visible), the stone structure of *c*.100 was originally 96 metres north-south by 87 metres east-west. The inner arena wall stood 3.4 metres high, the outer 26 metres high. The seating capacity was eight thousand.

b. Fortress wall. Foundations of the south-east angle and interval tower.

c. 'Roman Gardens', containing columns, a hypocaust and other building fragments removed from St Michael's Row in 1863.

d. Kaleyards. Foundations of the fortress wall outside the present city wall.

e. North Wall. Remains of the fortress wall with moulded cornice reconstructed *c*.300. Best seen from the canal towpath or George Street.

f. Abbey Green. Inside the north wall, the well-preserved remains of an interval tower and rampart buildings, including bread ovens.

g. Goss Street. Column base from the external colonnade on the west side of the *principia*.

h. Roodee. Remains of quay wall.

i. Handbridge. In Edgar's Field, a public garden on the south side of the Dee, is a Roman quarry face and a badly weathered figure, allegedly of Minerva — a quarrymen's shrine.

There are also three sites visible in the basements of shops in the city: **14 Northgate Row** contains the remnants of an isolated hypocaust; **23 Northgate Row** contains the massive base of one of the columns of the headquarters building and the ends of two other columns which project from the cellar walls; **39 Bridge Street** contains the remains of a well-preserved hypocaust showing part of the floor and its supports.

CLEVELAND

1. Huntcliff: signal station   NZ 687219
Along the clifftop footpath eastwards from Saltburn at 672216.

This signal station stands at the edge of an almost vertical cliff with magnificent views over Tees Bay and beyond. Only the southern third survives, the other parts having been carried away by coastal erosion. The outer defence is a V-shaped ditch 8.5 metres wide and 1.8 metres deep, with an entrance on the south. Inside this is a rectangular stone wall with semicircular projecting bastions for artillery at the corner angles. The wall is about 1.2 metres thick and still stands 0.9 metres high in places. There is a gateway 2.3 metres wide aligned on the ditch causeway. The interior courtyard was roughly paved. Only a portion of the south wall of the central tower survives, representing a building 15 metres square. Between the gateway and the tower was a well 1.8 metres across and 4.3 metres deep. In the filling of this well were the bodies of fourteen adults and children, probably the occupants of the station who had been slaughtered and flung down the well when the stronghold was overrun at the end of the fourth century or later.

CORNWALL

1. Breage: milestone   SW 618285
In the parish church.

This milestone is dedicated to the Emperor Postumus (258-68). Like the St Hilary example (Cornwall, 4) it is not associated with any known Roman road, and both are probably related to a switch of most of the Roman tin trade from Spain to Cornwall between *c.* 240 and 310.

2. Carn Euny: village and fogou   SW 403288
Approach by a byroad north from Brane, which is reached from the A30 at Lower Drift.

This is a Roman continuation of a village of timber-built huts dating from the fourth century BC. These were replaced by stone-built courtyard houses from the first century onwards. The *fogou* (underground stone-lined passage), unusual in having a circular side chamber with a corbelled roof, is probably pre-Roman in origin but may have continued in use well into the Roman period. A leaflet guide has been published.

7. *Chysauster, Cornwall: the clustered huts.*

3. Chysauster: village   SW 472350
By the B3311, turning at Badger's Cross (486332), taking the road north-west, or other signposted turnings in the area.

Chysauster is the classic example of this Romano-British village type, which originated in the iron age. The site comprises eight courtyard houses arranged in pairs along a street. To the south-east is a ruined fogou, and there is a field system nearby. It is uncertain whether Castle-an-Dinas hillfort, on the hill to the east (485350), was a defensive stronghold serving this village in times of unrest. The site is maintained by English Heritage and a detailed guide, card guide and postcards are normally available.

4. St Hilary: milestone   SW 551313
In the parish church.

This milestone is dedicated to the Emperor Constantine the Great as Caesar (306-8). For its probable significance, see Breage (Cornwall, 1).

5. Trevelgue Head: cliff-castles   SW 827630
By the footpath west of the B3276, just north of St Columb Porth near Newquay.

The two castles (or parts of the same castle) are linked by a footbridge and situated on a promontory overlooking Newquay. There are four ramparts to the east and two to the west of this bridge. Excavation just before the Second World War revealed foundations of a large circular house 14 metres in diameter, occupied from c.200 BC to AD 120, and the finds included coins of Vespasian and Trajan. The site is easy of access and under grass.

CUMBRIA

Eight sites in this county are described in the section on Hadrian's Wall. They are: Appletree, Banks Burn, Banks East, Birdoswald, Coombe Crag, Maryport, Ravenglass and Willowford (pages 73-6).

1. Ambleside *Galava*: fort   NY 373034
The site lies in Borrans Fields on the south side of the road linking the A591 and A593. It belongs to the National Trust and is signposted.

The visible remains are of the stone fort built in the second century and occupied until the fourth. It was excavated in 1913-15 and 1920 and is now hard to trace. Two gates, some of the angle towers and the central buildings of the fort were left exposed after the excavations but were not properly consolidated. The exposed remains were preceded by a clay and timber fort on slightly offset lines. Pottery from this phase dates from c. AD 90.

2. Crosby Garrett: settlement   NY 719064
Take the metalled track leading north-east from Newbiggin on the A685. Follow to 719061 and then cross the disused railway line. The settlement is a short distance to the north.

The settlement consists of three villages bounded by their field systems, together covering 65 hectares. The main village, on the south-east slope of Begin Hill, consists of a series of hut enclosures and associated paddocks on the south and west sides. On the south side of the village is an oblong building with stone doorposts *in situ*. A second village lies 650 metres north-east, with similar hut groups and paddocks, but is only half the size of the first. 275 metres north-east of this is a third village, comparable in size with the second. The three villages and their field systems are all part of a composite whole, but as yet no excavations have been undertaken and nothing is known of the groups occupying the sites.

3. Ewe Close, Crosby Ravensworth: settlement   NY 610135
Turn right by the telephone box in Crosby Ravensworth, then first

left by the post office. Bear left at the fork and follow it for 2.5 km until it ends in a farm. Go through the farmyard and a gate on the left, cross a stream and go through a gate ahead following a field wall on the right to the hilltop. The site is in the field beyond.

Ewe Close is a rather confused site consisting of a series of complicated earthworks probably representing several confluent farmsteads lining the Roman road which passes 18 metres to the west of the complex. The remains include a few hut circles and a series of flattened ridges.

4. Hardknott, Eskdale *Mediobogdum*: fort　　　NY 218015
Take the minor road leading east from Boot to Hardknott Pass. The fort and a small car park are to the north of the road. The site belongs to the National Trust.

The fort, built under Trajan, commands a dramatic position on a south-western spur of Hardknott between Eskdale and Hardknott valleys. The square fortification covers 1.2 hectares with gates in the centres of its four stone walls. The west, south and east gates were double-portalled, the north single. Internal buildings so far cleared included the *principia* and two granaries. To the south of the fort is a small bath block with the usual series of small rooms. North-east of the fort is a 1.2 hectares levelled area, evidently the parade ground, with a large *tribunal* on its north side.

5. Maiden Castle, Stainmore: fortlet　　　NY 872132
The site is a short distance north of the A66.

The site of this small 0.1 hectare fortlet commands a superb view of the descent to the Eden valley and was part of the Stainmore Pass defensive system. Two further stations are visible — Roper Castle and Bowes Moor (Durham, 3). The fortlet is surrounded by a stone wall 1.8 metres thick. It was built in the second century and occupied until the fourth.

6. Temple Sowerby: milestone　　　NY 620265
The milestone is on the verge of a lay-by on the north side of the A66 and is protected by an iron cage.

Apart from the better-preserved example at Chesterholm (Hadrian's Wall, 13, illustration 26), this is the only Roman milestone in Britain remaining in its original position. It still stands some 1.4 metres high.

DERBYSHIRE

1. Melandra Castle *Ardotalia*: fort　　　SK 008951
Take the track leading up the hillside north-west of the church at Brookfield on the A57, 3 km north-west of Glossop.

Well-sited on a tongue of high ground sloping steeply to the north and west, the fort was built to command the road from Brough (*Navio*) over the Snake Pass into Longdendale. Founded *c*. AD 78, it was abandoned *c*.140. The original clay rampart, reinforced by a stone wall and gateways soon after 100, enclosed 2 hectares. These defences are still very impressive. Excavations have revealed the plan of the *principia* and the timber barracks. Outside the north-west corner of the fort was a small bath-house, under investigation since 1973. Traces of timber structures in the nearby civil settlement have also been recorded. Other extra-mural settlement east and south-east of the fort was uncovered between 1966 and 1969. The focal point of this was a large wooden *mansio*. The whole settlement was protected by a ditch and bank which cut off access to the military zone from the south.

DEVON

1. Exeter *Isca Dumnoniorum*   SX 920926

Excavations have revealed parts of a legionary fortress of about 15 hectares within the area enclosed by the later town walls, the approximate centre being the crossroads of the present Fore Street, High Street, North Street and South Street, and the defences of this fortress served the town until the late second century, when the area of the town was extended to the line of the present town walls.

Within this area a settlement developed which extended to the region of the present Cathedral Close, where excavations west of the cathedral in 1971-7 revealed a legionary bath-house, subsequently incorporated into the *basilica* and adjoining forum. It is planned eventually to display them under a covered building. The Rougemont House Museum also contains a section of mosaic floor from a house in Catherine Street and other finds from Roman Exeter.

About AD 80 the military withdrew, leaving *Isca* an open city and the administrative centre of the Dumnonii of Cornwall, Devon and probably west Somerset, connected by the Fosse Way with towns to the north-east including Ilchester, Bath and Cirencester. A forum and a *basilica* were developed, and excavations since the Second World War have revealed evidence of dwellings and industries.

In the later second century the town was fortified by a rampart with outer ditch, broken by the north, east, south and west gates. In the early third century the rampart was cut back and faced with a massive wall, most of which remains today. These walls are still visible around most of their circuit but were in several places refurbished or altered in medieval or later times. They are well seen in Northernhay Gardens around Rougemont Castle, between Post Office Street and Southernhay West, and between South Gate and the river Exe. They enclose about 38 hectares.

On the occasion of the Silver Jubilee of Queen Elizabeth II in 1977 metal plaques were placed on certain walls to draw attention to significant archaeological features, including the sites of the Roman *basilica* and bath-house, and the Roman and later wall in Southernhay. The south gate Roman tower is marked out on the pavement in South Street opposite Holy Trinity church. The plinth of the Roman wall is exceptionally well preserved just south of this point.

2. Martinhoe: fortlet   SS 663493

By the road from the A39 at Martinhoe Cross (685464) to the north-west through and beyond Martinhoe village, then on foot across two fields.

On the coastal fringe of Exmoor, this early Roman fortlet comprises inner and outer enclosures, the entrance to the outer being on the landward side, and that to the inner on the seaward side, thereby exposing any attackers to fire from the defenders (as at Old Burrow, below). The Martinhoe fortlet was built *c.* AD 58-60 and contained barrack buildings adequate for the accommodation of from 65 to 80 troops under a centurion. It was abandoned *c.*75 when the founding of the legionary fortress at Caerleon rendered it no longer necessary as a point for watching the Bristol Channel and the Silures of South Wales. Finds from the excavation are in the Athenaeum Museum, Barnstaple.

3. Old Burrow: fortlet   SS 788493

Approach by the path from Black Gate, north-west of County Gate on the A39 between Lynmouth and Porlock. There is no public right of access.

On the coast of Exmoor, this early Roman fortlet comprises inner and outer enclosures; the entrance to the outer enclosure is on the landward side, and the entrance to the inner enclosure on the seaward side to confuse any attackers (as at Martinhoe, above). A bleakly situated site of a temporary character, with its occupants living in tents, it was built *c.* AD 48 to enable a watch to be kept on the Bristol Channel and the Silures of South Wales. It was abandoned *c.* AD 52 after the defeat of Caratacus and the Silures. A few years later it was replaced by the Martinhoe fortlet. Finds from excavations are in Taunton Museum.

4. Sourton: fortlet or signal station   SX 546919

A few yards west of the A386, south-west of Okehampton; shown on Ordnance Survey maps as a tumulus.

Behind the Roebuck Hotel and under pasture, this is a square earthwork with rounded corners, about 20 metres across. There are possible traces of a Roman road running southwest-northeast, just to the west.

DORSET

1. Ackling Dyke: road   SU 022178 to ST 967032
From the A354 the Roman road extends SSW to Badbury Rings. For the best portion, park at 016163 or 007144.

This is among the finest stretches of Roman road in Britain. By far the best and easiest part to explore is between Oakley Down and Wyke Down. It cuts through two of the early bronze age disc barrows on Oakley Down, is crossed by the B3081 on Handley Hill and cuts across the neolithic Dorset Cursus at 010152. For some miles in this area the road is between 12 and 15 metres wide and at least 1.8 metres high and provides a wonderful walk. It can be followed on foot for nearly 16 km to Badbury Rings, either on top of the *agger* or along the path on its east side.

2. Badbury Rings: hillfort, settlement and road junction
ST 964030
The B3082 between Blandford and Wimborne passes just to the south. Car park available.

The great multivallate hillfort has never been excavated. The convergence of four Roman roads immediately to the north implies some kind of settlement, and there is a small enclosed Roman settlement between the west side of the Rings and the Roman road to Dorchester. It may have had some administrative function akin to the similarly situated *Sorviodunum* (Old Sarum). The other Roman roads lead to *Sorviodunum*, towards Bath, and via a recently discovered first-century legionary base at Lake (ST 999991) to Hamworthy, where there were Roman potteries. The round barrows beside the Roman road to Dorchester, formerly claimed as Roman, are bronze age. The Roman name for this site is believed to have been *Vindocladia*.

3. Cerne Giant: hill figure   ST 667016
On the hillside, east of the A352 near Cerne Abbas. National Trust property.

This hill figure, of a giant wielding a knobbed club, is 55 metres high and 51 metres wide. There is no evidence of date, but the figure has been plausibly referred to the period of the Emperor Commodus (180-93), who posed as the incarnation of Hercules and assumed the title of Hercules Romanus. It has been suggested that it might be a representation of the Celtic Jupiter and belong to the pre-Roman iron age, but this seems less probable. There is a distinct possibility of a post-Roman date.

Comparison of the earliest known illustrations (dating from 1764) with the present figure shows that in the course of periodic scourings and renovations the navel has become added to the length of the phallus. The only comparable hill figure in southern England is the Long Man of Wilmington (East Sussex, 2, illustration 49).

4. Combs Ditch: linear earthwork ST 851021 to 887000
The A354 between Dorchester and Blandford cuts across this earthwork at 857018.

This linear ditch has its rampart on the south-west and in its final form functioned as a defence against an attack expected from the north-east. The length is about 4 miles (6.5 km) and it covers the neck of land between the Winterborne stream and the river Stour. It probably originated as an iron age boundary ditch but was strengthened in the late Roman or sub-Roman period for defence.

5. Dorchester *Durnovaria* SY 693907

It is believed that, following the conquest of the native occupants of Maiden Castle (Dorset, 9) in about AD 44, a military post, or fort, probably with a small civilian settlement associated, was established somewhere in the higher part of the present town, where Roman military equipment has been found; but so far no traces of the actual fort have been located. This was succeeded, *c*. AD 70, by a civilian town which served as the *civitas* capital of the Durotriges. During the fourth century this function was shared with *Lindinis* (Ilchester) (Somerset, 4).

In the middle or late second century the town was enclosed by defences comprising a rampart with outer ditches. On the west and south sides these are followed by The Grove, West Walk, Bowling Alley and South Walk. It is uncertain to what extent this rampart continued along the natural scarp following the north-east boundary above the river Frome. About 300 a stone wall and parapet were added in front of these ramparts. The core of a short stretch of this wall is exposed south of the West Gate and the Hardy statue. A rectilinear street grid was planned parallel to the west and south walls.

The public baths, near Woolaston House, were recently located and excavated but are no longer exposed to view. No other public buildings have yet been located within the town. Outside the south-west corner is the impressive amphitheatre, known as **Maumbury Rings** (SY 690899), between the two railway stations. Originally a neolithic 'henge' monument, this was, per-

8. *Dorchester, Dorset: the Roman city wall.*

haps in the second century or soon afterwards, converted into an amphitheatre about 107 metres in diameter, with an entrance at the north-east and a performers' enclosure at the south-west end.

9. *Dorchester, Dorset: the town-house in Colliton Park.*

The earthwork was altered and reused during the Civil War.

Water supply was provided by the fine aqueduct in the form of a chalk-cut channel lined with clay, extending from the river Frome near Maiden Newton to a high level point near the West Gate, whence the water was distributed throughout the town.

Durnovaria possesses, within its north-west corner, between the County Hall and the river Frome, in the area known as **Colliton Park**, an L-shaped fourth-century town house. It includes a room with a geometrical mosaic still in place. This and other mosaics (some in the Dorset County Museum) from the town and surrounding countryside suggest that the town had its own school of mosaicists.

Cemeteries include one at **Fordington**, whose church of St George contains an inscribed Roman tombstone of Purbeck marble; another was discovered during the building of Thomas Hardy's House at Max Gate to the south-east; and there was an almost entirely Christian cemetery of more than a thousand graves on the east side of Poundbury to the north-west.

Durnovaria is connected by Roman roads to a probable harbour at Radipole near Weymouth, Exeter, Ilchester, and via Badbury Rings to *Sorviodunum* and beyond (see Stinsford, Dorset, 10).

6. Hod Hill: garrison fort within earlier hillfort ST 857106
Turn off the A350 near Steepleton House at 861110, where there is a lay-by, and then walk up the public footpath to the south-west.

The iron age hillfort of 20 hectares had a long and complex history before its capture during the conquest phase in AD 44, when a Roman garrison fort was built within its north-west and highest part. It was garrisoned by a legionary detachment of about six hundred men and an auxiliary cavalry unit of about two hundred and fifty men. The garrison fort encloses nearly 2.8 hectares, and excavation during the 1950s revealed foundations of the *principia*, the commandant's house, barrack blocks for infantry and cavalry and a latrine with ten compartments. The fort was partly destroyed by fire in about AD 51 and abandoned then or very soon afterwards. Most of the finds are in the British Museum.

7. Jordon Hill: temple   SY 699821
Take the minor road off the A353 at Overcombe (696816); turn left after 400 metres and park beyond the houses.

The hill is crowned by the partially preserved foundations of what was probably a double-square Romano-Celtic temple, excavated in 1843 and 1932. At its south-east corner was a shaft filled

10. *Hod Hill, Dorset: the Roman camp occupies one corner of the iron age hillfort.*

with sixteen deposits which appear to have been ritual, as each comprised bones of birds with a Roman bronze coin placed between flat slabs. The building may date from the early fourth century and it continued in use until about 400. Capitals and bases of Tuscan columns suggest that it was a building of some quality. It is under the guardianship of English Heritage. There was an extensive cemetery nearby.

8. Kingston Down: settlement and field system
SY 957780 (centre)

Approach by the path from the B3069 at Kingston, leading to Chapman's Pool.

This is an area of about 60 hectares in close proximity to areas where Kimmeridge shale was worked for lathe-turned furniture, tableware etc, Purbeck marble for monumental inscriptions and architectural decoration, and Purbeck stone for more modest uses. A Roman altar of Purbeck marble from this locality is in Dorset County Museum.

9. Maiden Castle: Roman temple inside iron age hillfort
SY 669884

Access by road south-west of Dorchester and then a short walk.

A multi-phase and multivallate hillfort, Maiden Castle in its final form enclosed 19 hectares. Its last British occupants, the Durotriges, were in *c*. AD 43 overthrown when the hillfort was stormed by the II Augustan Legion under the future Emperor Vespasian. The bodies of some of the vanquished were buried in a 'war cemetery' within the outworks of the eastern entrance. In the Dorset County Museum is a grim illustration of this event, a Roman iron ballista bolt embedded in the vertebra of a Durotrigan defender.

Within the eastern part of the hillfort a double-square Romano-Celtic temple was built after 367 and continued in use until well after 400. Among the finds from an excavation of 1882-4, the subject of Thomas Hardy's 'Tryst at an Ancient Earthwork', was a bronze plaque with a figure of Minerva. To the north-east are the remains of a two-roomed building interpreted as the 'priest's house' and to the south-west are foundations of an oval structure which contained cult objects and was probably a shrine.

10. Stinsford: milestone
SY 709914

On the roadside verge at the junction of the A35 and the minor road to Stinsford village.

This uninscribed milestone has been moved a little way from its original position beside the Roman road from Dorchester to Badbury Rings (Dorset, 2). The *agger* of this road can be seen 400 metres further on, beyond the village and at the left of the modern road. At 718916 the two part company, and the Roman road can be picked up again 2.4 km further on in **Thorncombe Wood**. For this, park by Hardy's Cottage and follow the display maps in the forest.

11. Woodcuts: settlement   ST 964182
Follow the B3081 westwards from Sixpenny Handley for about 2.4 km; immediately past the left turning signposted to Dean and Cashmoor, take the lane to the right. 800 metres on this reaches the earthworks on Woodcuts Common.

This circular earthwork, originally surmounted by a palisade, contained a large circular hut and some eighty grain storage pits (in use a few at a time). Built a few decades before the Roman conquest, this small farm continued virtually unchanged until the late second century, when more Romanised tastes appear in the artefacts and the use of wall plaster. Roman technology is evidenced by corn driers built in a small enclosure added to the main one, and by two wells that are now marked out in stone. After further alterations to the earthworks in the later third century this tiny settlement was abandoned, for unknown reasons, during the fourth century.

This site, like the others in Cranborne Chase, was thoroughly excavated in 1884 by the famous pioneer excavator General Pitt-Rivers, who subsequently restored the earthworks. A couple of miles away, across the county boundary, are two further settlement sites, Berwick Down and Rotherley (Wiltshire, 2).

DURHAM

1. Binchester *Vinovia*: fort   NZ 208318
The site lies due north of Bishop Auckland, beside a minor road leading north to Newfield. Park by the Binchester Hall Hotel.

This once large fort, of which the ramparts to north and east can still be traced, was occupied from AD 79 to 122 and then abandoned until *c*.160, when it was reoccupied. The spectacular hypocaust displayed under a protective building belonged to the bath suite of the commandant's house and dates from the fourth century. It is one of the best so far discovered in Britain. Note the tiles stamped *N CON* (the *numerus* of the Conganienses). Outside the building further rooms are under excavation for public display; it is clear that by the end of the fourth century they were converted to more mundane uses, including a forge and slaughterhouse. The substantial *vicus* outside the fort is not now visible.

2. Bowes *Lavatris*: fort   NY 990134
The site is immediately to the west of Bowes village.

This fort, which guarded the eastern end of the Stainmore Pass, is now much overgrown. It was heavily quarried for materials to build the church and Norman castle. The church is within the northern boundary of the fort and the churchyard in the north-east corner, while the modern extension to the latter lies in the eastern end. The fort's ditches are still visible except where the castle moat obliterates them at the northern end. An entrance stood west of centre on the south side, and the northern one may be marked by the line of the vicarage lane. The defences — a stone wall, bank and ditch — enclosed an area of 1.7 hectares in the early third century, and finds suggest an occupation between Agricola and the late fourth century. In the nineteenth century an aqueduct was found; this carried water to the fort from Laverpool, 3 km away. A bath-house was found outside the south-east corner of the defences. It was partially dug in the nineteenth century and measures 9.1 by 6.1 metres, with a southern entrance. Its position is now marked by an overgrown depression.

3. Bowes: signal station   NY 929125
The site is immediately north of the A66, west of Bowes and near the Bowes Moor Hotel.

Situated at the mouth of the Stainmore Pass, this station is part of the pass communications system established in the second half of the second century. An intermediate signal station between here and the fort of *Lavatris* (Durham, 2) is not now visible on the ground; the next station to the west, Roper Castle, is clearly visible on the skyline (in Cumbria). The Bowes station is 18 by 14 metres and consists of a V-shaped ditch 3 metres wide and a 3 metres turf rampart. This enclosure was straight-sided, the angles rounded externally and squared on the inner face. There is no trace of the central timber tower.

4. Ebchester *Vindomora*: fort   NZ 102557
The site is at Mains Farm, at the edge of the village and on a byroad off the A694. Turn off the main road by the bus shelter near the church, to the farm, where there is a small museum.

The fort began as a turf and timber structure *c.* AD 80. It was rebuilt in stone in the second century, abandoned in 140 , then reoccupied from 163 to 400, with a major rebuilding *c.*300. The only visible remnant is a hypocaust in an apse-shaped room, perhaps part of the commandant's bath suite. The walls and supporting stone pillars are still some 0.9 metres high. Excavation has shown that the heating system went out of use by the end of the third century.

5. Greta Bridge *Maglona*: fort   NZ 085132
Turn off the A66 at the Morritt Arms Hotel, on the Brignall road.

The hotel is built over the northern part of the site and the visible remains are in the first field on the left.

The existing earthworks are the southern defences of the fort, which is undated and virtually unexcavated. The earthen rampart is conspicuous and the twin ditches forming the defences can be clearly traced. When the bypass was built, timber buildings of the *vicus* were discovered, indicating occupation from the early second century to the end of the third.

6. Piercebridge *Magis*(?): fort and bridge   NZ 208156

The fort is on the south-west side of the village.

The village lies largely within the 4.4 hectares fort, built presumably on or near the site of earlier forts in the fourth century to the west of the Roman bridge taking Watling Street across the Tees. Extensive excavations in the 1970s have elucidated much of the history of the site. The remains of the Roman bridge were found in a nearby gravel quarry and subsequently consolidated by the Department of the Environment. A solidly built barrack block belonging to the fourth-century phase of the fort was uncovered in 1973-4. Further operations have revealed an internal bathhouse with latrine and hot and cold rooms. The ditch of the fort is also under investigation. At the north end of the village, beyond and to the right of the Wheatsheaf Inn, the masonry of the corner of the fort wall is well preserved, with an internal latrine.

11. Piercebridge, Durham: the remains of the Roman bridge.

7. Rey Cross: marching camp   NY 900124

On the A66 at the summit of Stainmore Pass, the road passes through the site from east to west, and there is a lay-by on the left.

Part of the southern half of the western defences of this fine marching camp has been quarried away, and some of the north rampart has slid into a bog. The other ramparts average 1.8 metres in height and are 6 metres wide; as the underlying rock is near the surface, the ditch was omitted. No less than nine gates survive, each protected by a *titulum*, and two further gates have probably been obliterated by the road. The camp could hold a full legion and may have protected the IX Legion during the Brigantian campaign of AD 72-3.

8. Scargill: shrines   NY 998105

Take the bridlepath leading south of the minor road to Bowes at 992124. The path leads to a footbridge over Eller Beck. The shrines are on the hillside above the bridge.

The first of these two Roman shrines is a rectangular platform cut into the hillside and lined with dressed masonry. It is 4 metres across and 1.8 metres deep. Set centrally against the back wall is an altar dedicated by Julius Secundus, centurion of the First Cohort of Thracians, to the god Silvanus, and dating to the third century. The second shrine is 15 metres to the south-east. It consists of a circular masonry wall 5.2 metres across, with the remains of a stone bench inside. Fragments of seven altars were found here, the finest (now in the Bowes Museum, Barnard Castle) being of sandstone, dedicated by Frontinus, prefect of the First Cohort of Thracians, to the god of hunting, Vinotonus/ Silvanus, and dating to the third century.

ESSEX

1. Bartlow Hills: barrows   TL 586448

Approach from near the now closed Bartlow railway station by a signposted footpath from the road between Bartlow and Ashdon. A good picnic spot.

Only four of originally eight steep-sided barrows still exist; one beyond the railway line can be seen only from the other barrows. When built, the barrows ran from north to south in two lines of four mounds each. The western line of smaller barrows was destroyed in 1832. The larger eastern mounds still stand and are the most magnificent barrows in Britain. It is probable that they were the family tombs of Romano-British dignitaries living in the district in the early second century AD. They were dug into between 1832 and 1840. Unfortunately almost all the objects found were destroyed in a fire in 1847.

From north to south the contents of the surviving barrows were:
1. Inaccessible, beyond the railway line. A bronze bowl and strigil, and an iron lamp.
2. 7.6 metres high, on the southern edge of the railway line. A wooden chest in the centre held a glass jug and pottery jar, both of which contained cremated bones. A bronze jug and basin, another iron lamp, samian pottery and the petals of a flower.
3. 12 metres high and 44 metres in diameter. Built of alternate layers of earth and chalk. A tunnel was driven into the centre by John Gale, who found a cavity left by a decayed wooden chest that had measured 1.27 by 1.12 by 0.61 metres. In it were a glass jar containing cremated bones, three glass jugs holding liquids, two long-necked perfume bottles, two bronze strigils, decorated bronze jugs and an elaborate casket enamelled in red, green and blue. One of the most interesting items was a folding iron 'camp' stool with bronze fittings and a seat, which was identified by Michael Faraday (the pioneer of electricity) as made of leather. Leaning against the outside of the chest was a globular wine jar containing more cremated bones.
4. 11 metres high (rather overgrown; closest to the road). Another wooden chest was found placed on a chalk floor, containing cremated bones in a glass urn. A bronze jug decorated with a lion's head and a saucepan with an elaborate handle seem to have been wrapped in a piece of linen. A samian dish contained chicken bones, part of a funeral feast perhaps. The tomb also contained an iron lamp with a wreath of box leaves wrapped around its handle.

The barrow cemetery may once have been enclosed within an earthwork, traces of which have been found running north-east of the mounds towards the river Granta.

There is a small museum in Bartlow, but the surviving objects from the barrows are in the Saffron Walden Museum.

2. Bradwell *Othona*: fort   TL 031082
Follow the Roman road for almost 3 km north-east of Bradwell-on-Sea. This track can be very muddy in wet weather.

Very little of the three sides of this badly damaged fort of the Saxon Shore now survives. The south wall is best preserved. It stands some 1.2 to 1.5 metres high and is 3.7 metres thick. It lies to the south of the church. Excavation has shown that the fort was not quite rectangular. It was 158 metres long, but its width is not known as the eastern wall has been destroyed by the sea. The interior of the fort is under cultivation. It has been tentatively identified as *Othona*, listed in the *Notitia Dignitatum*, and was probably founded under Carausius in 286-93, although earlier finds have come from the site.

On the line of the west wall of the fort, close to the North Sea, stands the lonely chapel of St Peter-on-the-Wall. This is probably the actual church built by St Cedd about 654. Only a nave now stands although an apsed chancel and west porch have been traced. Much Roman material is incorporated in the building.

3. Colchester *Camulodunum*   TL 995253 (centre)

Camulodunum was probably the capital of Addedomarus, ruler of the iron age tribe of the Trinovantes. Shortly after 10 BC the capital was captured by the Catuvellauni under their leader Tasciovanus, who minted coins marked *CAMV* there. The conquest was short-lived, and Addedomarus reappeared, followed by Dubnovellaunus of Kent. However, by about AD 10 Cunobelin, son of Tasciovanus, had acquired the Trinovantian throne and ruled the whole of south-east England from *Camulodunum* until his death about AD 42.

The iron age capital was a large promontory fortress, enclosing some 31 square km and bounded on the north, south and east by the Roman River and the river Colne. The western defences were supplied by a number of lines of dykes spanning the 5 km between the rivers.

12. Plan of Colchester showing the sites described in the text: a, Temple of Claudius; b, Balkerne Gate; c, North Gate; d, Holly Trees Meadow; e, Priory Street; f, postern gate; g, theatre; h, church.

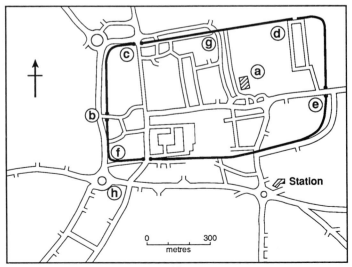

This capital surrendered to the Emperor Claudius in AD 43. Six years later it was created *Colonia Claudia* (*Victricensis* being added, probably after the revolt of Boudicca in 61). On Claudius' death and deification in 54 a great classical temple (a) dedicated to him was begun, on a huge masonry base 32 by 24 metres and 3.4 metres high, with a further 4 metres below ground. It was incomplete at the time of the Boudiccan revolt but was subsequently finished in a modified form with the customary precinct. The superstructure was destroyed by the Normans, who used the vaulted substructure as a base for the castle. These vaults still exist and are shown in conducted tours. The castle itself now contains the fine Colchester and Essex Museum. Over twenty years of patient excavation have pieced together the evolution of Roman Colchester from an initial legionary fort with bank, ditch and timber buildings. This next became the first *colonia*, with civilians now living in converted barrack blocks while prestigious public buildings (such as the temple) were being built outside it. By AD 60 the town was spreading eastwards and lacked effective defences when the Boudiccan revolt broke out; numerous discoveries of burnt timbers, clay, pottery and glass, particularly in the western part of the town, attest to the catastrophic nature of the sacking.

The town was rebuilt and extended after the revolt, but still without substantial defences; for the fine stone walls were not

13. Colchester, Essex: one of the vaults of the temple of Claudius, under the Norman castle.

added until the second century, probably in two stages, to be followed a generation later by the addition of an internal bank. This is an exceptionally early date for stone walls and it reverses the usual sequence for earthen and masonry phases. These walls still survive for most of their length and enclose 44 hectares. There were at least six gateways, of which the most famous is the Balkerne Gate (b) on the western side of the Roman town. It was probably an early monumental arch, later incorporated into the defences. Two arches survive, and its northern tower reaches 6 metres in height. It originally had two large arches for traffic and smaller pedestrian arches on either side with D-shaped bastions holding guardrooms. The foundations of half of it now lie under the King's Head Inn. From the Balkerne Gate it is possible to walk the circuit of the surviving portions of the Roman Walls in about an hour.

Leaving the Balkerne Gate on your right, walk down Balkerne Hill, where the wall is in good condition, built of alternate layers of tiles and *septaria* (clay nodules from the London clay). The northern angle of the wall sweeps widely round to North Gate (c). Nothing of this entrance survives above ground level, nor of the next gate, Rye Gate. The wall reappears along Park Follet and is well seen inside the Castle Park. At the north-east corner of Holly Trees Meadow was a small gate, whose excavated remains can still be seen (d). Outside the wall beyond this point is a good section of the great ditch which must have run all round the town. The rounded north-east corner of the wall can be seen, but the next section is much damaged as it passes on to Dobson's Meadow.

The East Gate was demolished in 1651 and 1657. In an alley on the east side of St James's churchyard can be seen part of the wall containing the outlet of a Roman drain. The wall continues in Priory Street (e), where it can now best be seen, and again in Vineyard Street. In places it has been patched, and bastions added, probably during the reign of Richard I. No Roman gate is known to have existed at Scheregate, which was medieval. Head Gate must have had a Roman foundation corresponding with the North Gate, although nothing can be seen today. The south-east angle of the town wall was destroyed after the siege of 1648, but in Balkerne Lane it can be seen once more in excellent condition almost to parapet level. In the wall on the north of St Mary's Steps can be seen part of the arch of a narrow postern gate (f) 760 mm wide and about 2.4 metres high.

In Maidenburgh Street can now be seen part of the theatre (g), successor to that mentioned by Tacitus and identified in 1981. Part of its masonry is incorporated into St Helen's Chapel, part in a modern building on the site, and more marked out in modern coloured bricks.

14. Colchester, Essex: the fourth-century cemetery church

Next to the Butt Road police station (h) can now be seen the restored foundations of a fourth-century building. This is thought to have been a church associated with an extramural cemetery (illustration 14).

Several town-houses had mosaic floors, some of which are now in the museum, with a model of the temple and two famous military tombstones of a centurion and a cavalryman.

4. Harlow: temple   TL 468124
The site is on the northern edge of Harlow New Town, between the river Stort and the railway line west of the station.

The site was excavated in 1927 and again in 1962-71 and is now marked out on the site. The temple is of the usual concentric square Romano-Celtic plan, with a *cella* surrounded by an ambulatory, enclosed by a precinct wall with an ornamental gateway, an altar and other buildings. The site was clearly venerated in the later iron age, to judge from the valuable, and presumably dedicatory, finds. The first actual temple of AD 75-100 was in stone with a timber palisade; the remodelling, with the precinct wall and ancillary buildings, belongs to the third century. Worship continued into the fourth century, demonstrating (as at Lydney, Gloucestershire, 7, and elsewhere) the persistence of pagan cults into the Christian era. Apparently it eventually fell into disuse; there is no suggestion (as at Carrawburgh, Hadrian's Wall, 11, and London) of destruction by Christian activists.

5. Mersea Mount: chambered barrow   TM 023144
Immediately on entering Mersea island by the B1025 take the left

51

fork, the East Mersea road, for 800 metres. The barrow is railed off on the left.

This Romano-British barrow, 34 metres in diameter and 6.7 metres high, contains a brick vault, 475 mm square and 533 mm high, built of Roman tiles. Inside was found a lead casket protecting a glass bowl which held the cremated bones of an adult. They are now in Colchester Museum. When the barrow was opened in 1912 a passage was built into it giving access to the burial chamber. A key may be obtained from a house nearby.

The foundations of what may have been a Romano-British wheel tomb (i.e. its plan resembling the spokes of a wheel) could once be seen in a garden in Pharos Lane, West Mersea. Such structures are paralleled by numerous tombs in Italy, including the Mausoleum of Augustus. This site is no longer visible.

6. Sturmer: barrow   TL 688444

The barrow is 2 km south-east of Haverhill, on the south side of the A604.

Although ploughed, this barrow is still bold and clear, standing some 1.8 metres high. It was probably Roman: a late fourth-century coin hoard was found nearby, and the barrow stands near the head of the Stour valley with a Roman road passing close by.

GLOUCESTERSHIRE

1. Bury Hill Camp: hillfort and Roman settlement
ST 652791

Approach the site from the minor road at Moorend.

Many iron age hillforts continued to be used into the Roman period. This is well illustrated at Bury Hill. Two banks are separated by a single ditch from the defences of this pear-shaped hillfort of about 2 hectares. Quarrying for Pennant stone has removed the western part of the earthwork. There are three possible entrances, but later Roman occupation has obscured the iron age structure to some extent. A Roman well was found south of the north-west entrance.

The U-shaped ditch was 6.1 metres wide and 1.5 metres deep and provided a quarry for rubble to build the ramparts, which still stand 2.7 metres high in places and have a drystone retaining wall. Excavation in 1926 showed that most of the interior features are Romano-British, including a long mound near the centre, on the west side, which covers a house.

2. Chedworth: villa   SP 053134

This National Trust property is off the A429 at Fossebridge, signposted along the road from Yanworth to Withington. Car park and museum beside the villa.

This is the finest of more than a dozen Roman villas found within 16 km of Cirencester. It was discovered in 1864 and has since been extensively excavated. The site chosen was beside a spring in a small valley with wide views to the east. The villa began as a number of separate buildings along the sides and end of the valley in the first half of the second century AD. The original house stood at the end of the valley; it was smaller than at present and lacked the bath suite, which at that time stood apart, at the west end of what was to become the north wing. A small half-timbered building stood on the site of the south wing. This, together with the main house, was destroyed by fire and later restored, early in the third century. At the same time the north wing was extended and the bath-house enlarged. It was early in the fourth century that all the buildings were drawn together by the construction of a continuous corridor, which created an inner courtyard that would have contained a formal garden. This private part contrasted with the large courtyard, presumably a farmyard, to the east; this was enclosed by the long north and south wings, but any east wing and entrance have been lost through severe erosion, being at the downhill end of the site. On the south side of the western, private court and garden lay the kitchen and latrines and a room that jutted out into the garden. Beyond the kitchen was a furnace room which heated a large new dining room, which had mosaic pavements depicting the four seasons. This was situated at the south end of the west wing. At the north end of this wing a new small set of baths of classic Roman type was constructed. Adjoining these were two further rooms with mosaics, revealed in 1981 and scheduled for conservation and public display. The old baths in the north wing were reconstructed as *laconica,* with large cold plunges and a colonnade fronting the garden. For many years after the excavation these were mistaken for a fullery.

Beyond the north-west corner of the villa lies the spring which supplied water to the site. This was covered by a small apsidal building, the Nymphaeum. Inside was an octagonal basin which continually held 4,160 litres of water and once supplied the present house on the site. Other reservoirs would almost certainly have been needed to supplement the supply to such a large house. A further dining room and guest suite with hypocaust were added in the late fourth century, in the north wing, east of the baths. Nothing is now visible of the east end of the south wing, which is still unexcavated. Life in the villa seems to have come to an end late in the fourth century.

The original approach to the villa was from the White Way through the wood to the north-east. This track passed close to a barrow which produced the cremation urn now in the site museum. Close to the river Coln, 800 metres south-east of the villa, stood a square pagan temple, which produced the hunting relief also exhibited in the museum. There is a fine shop and visitors' centre. An illustrated guidebook is available.

3. Cirencester *Corinium Dobunnorum*: town   SP 0202
The Corinium Museum makes a splendid starting point, since there is not a great deal to see of the Roman town.

The Corinium Museum is one of the finest in Britain, with a clear and detailed history of the Roman town excellently displayed. Reconstructed rooms and a small garden bring to life a town that has not survived very well on the ground but has produced a wealth of archaeological material.

Cirencester began as a civilian settlement outside a small fort. The position was a good one at the junction of five important roads and a river crossing. However, the siting of the earliest fort on marshy ground at Watermoor was at fault, and it was soon moved 450 metres north to an area bounded by The Avenue, Chester Street, Watermoor Road and St Michael's Fields.

Not long after AD 60 a gradual movement of native tribesmen began from the Dobunnic centre, perhaps at Bagendon 5 km to the north, into the more attractive Romanised settlement. By about AD 75 the fort was dismantled, and all trace of it was buried beneath the expanding township, which became the tribal administrative centre for the Dobunni, *Corinium Dobunnorum*. A grid of streets was laid out, the position of which is still followed by Lewis Lane and Watermoor Road. A *forum* and *basilica* were constructed, as well as many shops and private houses. The position of walls forming the apse of the *basilica* is marked in a cul-de-sac which opens off the south-east side of The Avenue opposite Tower Street.

As the town developed during the second century an amphitheatre was constructed, first of timber and earth, later rebuilt in stone. It survives today and is known as the Bullring. Its grass-covered banks are 8.2 metres high and excavation has shown that they were originally terraced with low limestone walls which probably supported wooden seats. Two opposing entrance passages are still visible, that on the north being 29 metres long and lined with stone walls. The arena measures 49 by 41 metres. The amphitheatre can be reached by a path 230 metres from the old railway bridge in Cotswold Avenue.

Earthen defences with two external ditches and masonry towers were constructed during the second half of the second century, enclosing some 97 hectares. At the same time at least one gate (the Verulamium Gate), with twin semicircular towers and an

15. Cirencester, Gloucestershire: the 'Roman Garden' in the Corinium Museum.

adjoining bridge over the river Churn, was built on the road to St Albans and Leicester. About 220 the defences were strengthened by cutting back the earthen rampart and inserting a stone wall 3 metres thick; later, in the fourth century, external stone bastions were added. Parts of the earthen rampart and wall can now be seen north-west of London Road and in the Abbey Gardens, while a good section exists in The Beeches, Watermoor Gardens, south-east of London Road.

A number of changes occurred to the *forum* and *basilica* early in the fourth century, which may perhaps be explained by the promotion of the town to provincial capital. It is likely that life continued at *Corinium* until well into the fifth century and beyond. Indeed it is probable that part of the town survived at the time of the battle of Dyrham in 577, when four British kings were defeated and Cirencester fell into Saxon hands.

4. Gloucester *Glevum*: colonia   SO 8318

Gloucester was for long the base of the Twentieth Legion until AD 70 before it moved to Wroxeter (Shropshire, 1). Neither the legionary fortress of 17.4 hectares nor the slightly earlier and smaller fort at Kingsholm, 1.6 km to the north, is visible. The rapidly growing civilian population at first occupied the deserted legionary timber barracks, replacing them before long with stone houses. The resulting town was awarded the title *Colonia Nervia (na) Glevensium* under Nerva (AD 96-8) and flourished through the second century and beyond. Its first-century defences were

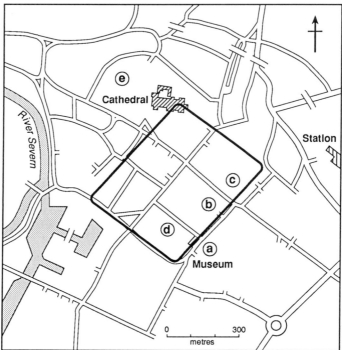

16. Plan of Gloucester showing the sites mentioned in the text: a, colonia wall; b, part of East Gate (Boots'); c, Eastgate Shopping Centre; d, Friends' Meeting House in Greyfriars; e, church of St Mary-de-Lode.

remodelled more than once, the latest being *c.*270-90.

The historical importance of *Glevum* is not reflected in the visibility of its remains. A length of the *colonia* wall is incorporated into the City Museum in Brunswick Road (a), which also contains some notable sculptures. Part of the East Gate can be visited in Boots' branch in Eastgate Street (b) during opening hours. Fragmentary mosaics from town-houses can be found in the Eastgate Shopping Centre (c), the National Westminster Bank in Eastgate Street, the Friends' Meeting House in Greyfriars (d) and (below a trapdoor) the church of St Mary-de-Lode (e) at the north-west of the cathedral precinct.

5. Great Witcombe: villa   SO 899142
The villa, open to the public, is signposted on the A417 400

metres east of the crossroads with the A46. It is 2.4 km south of the road along a rough track past Droy's Court. Cars may be parked in the farmyard. Key at the farm.

The beautiful site of this villa proved treacherous, as the hillside is riddled with springs and soil slip necessitated constant buttressing and rebuilding. Two rooms have been independently identified as shrines to the water spirits of the site: the prominent octagonal room in the middle (which replaced an earlier room) and one in the centre of the west wing with three niches and a central basin set in the floor. Two principal phases of the late third and fourth centuries are represented by the extensive remains of this H-shaped villa. The baths at the south-west corner belong to the later phase and are well preserved and displayed, with geometric and aquatic mosaics. The wall paintings were bright and gay, and small pots containing some of the paint were found during the excavations.

6. Littledean: temple (?) SO 675128

The site is in the grounds of Little Dean Hall, north of the road between Newnham (A48) and Littledean (A4151). Park at the end of the drive by the Hall. The site is accessible at all times, but permission should be sought.

This enigmatic building has been excavated and inaccurately conserved for display since 1984. It is on two levels: the lower

17. Great Witcombe villa, Gloucestershire.

has a rectangular *cella* with an ambulatory on three sides. The upper has the concentric square form of a typical Romano-Celtic temple. Much of the reconstruction is imaginative; in particular, both the apse at the west end with its drain and the water basin are spurious. The site lacked the copious dedicatory finds normal for a temple, but some material of the second and third centuries was found. It would thus be earlier than the temple complex at Lydney 12 km to the south-west. However, the Roman date proposed for the building itself has been questioned.

7. Lydney Park: hillfort, temple etc   SO 616027

Lydney Park is a private deer park and permission to visit must be sought in writing from the agent at Lydney Park Estate Office. Access is from the A48 at SO 623021 and through the farm.

This steep-sided iron age promontory fort encloses some 2 hectares and was constructed during the first century BC by erecting two banks with external ditches across the north-east end of the spur. There were probably two entrances: one at the southern tip of the spur, having inturned flanks, and a second at the southern limit of the earthworks on the east side. The gap in the north rampart is of recent origin. The inner bank on the east side is probably a later, but pre-Roman, addition.

The inhabitants seem to have spent uninterrupted lives until well into the fourth century AD, producing metalwork, including brooches, and mining iron on the site. Two iron mines have been found and one is visible, its entrance marked by a trapdoor, some 37 metres along the east side of the plateau, north of the Adam and Eve statues. It extends 15 metres underground and reaches a depth of 4.6 metres. It cuts through the iron age rampart, which was rebuilt over the gallery. The mine was being worked not later than the third century. Original pick marks can still be seen on the ferruginous walls of the mine. (Prospective visitors are warned to take protective clothing and torches.) The second mine lies under the Roman bath suite on the west side of the site.

Early in the fourth century the prehistoric rampart was partly rebuilt. Shortly after 364 a large temple with a guesthouse and bath suite was erected in the southern half of the hillfort. The temple, which measures 24 by 18 metres, was entered by a flight of steps from the south-east. These led into a 3 metre wide corridor or ambulatory which passed around the four sides of a rectangular *cella* which was divided into three smaller sanctuaries. Its present form is that of the rebuilding, *c.*367-75, after a collapse. In the ambulatory is a series of alcoves, or 'chapels' — a unique feature — each with a mosaic in front. The temple was dedicated to the British deity Nodens (or Nodons), who was connected with healing, sun and water. Evidently the temple and its cult continued into the later fourth century, demonstrating the persistence of pagan worship in rural areas when Christianity was the official religion.

The bath suite lies north of the temple. It was fed by a conduit from a water tank in the centre of the hillfort and contained the normal range of hot, warm and cold rooms. To the south of the baths lay a long, narrow building divided into compartments, which may have been cubicles for patients taking some form of health cure or lock-up shops where tourists could purchase votive offerings and souvenirs. The long verandah may reflect the classical practice of sleeping out in the expectation of a cure.

The final building in the group, an extensive guesthouse some 40 by 49 metres, is no longer visible.

Objects excavated from the iron age and Roman sites by Dr and Mrs R. E. M. Wheeler in 1928-9 are in the private museum in Lydney Park.

8. Spoonley Wood: villa   SP 045257

From Charlton Abbots take the minor road to Guiting Power. At the crossroads turn left (signposted Winchcombe); about 1 km on, a lane to the left leads to Spoonley Farm. The second track to the right after the farm enters a wood, continues as a footpath to the villa site. Permission should be sought at Charlton Abbots Manor.

This once fine villa might prove a disappointment after the effort of finding it. Excavated in the nineteenth century, at least three geometric mosaics, much damaged by tree roots, were lifted and their whereabouts is unknown. A fourth, however, was largely restored with modern materials and can still be found on the site. The overgrown walls of the villa can be traced with difficulty.

9. Wadfield: villa   SP 024261

Take the B4632 from Winchcombe to Cheltenham and after about 1 km take the minor road to Charlton Abbots and Brockhampton. Just beyond the sign to Belas Knap Long Barrow, park and take the public footpath on the left of the road. The site is in a small copse in the centre of a field. Permission should be sought at Charlton Abbots Manor 1.6 km along the road.

The nineteenth-century excavations were not properly backfilled, and the walls, although neglected and overgrown, can still be made out. Two ranges of rooms with a courtyard contained the bath suite to the south, and the main reception room with a fine geometric mosaic. This floor was vandalised by souvenir-hunters, but the better-preserved half was lifted and relaid for a while at Sudeley Castle. It was subsequently returned to the site, restored and covered with a wooden shed.

HADRIAN'S WALL

The Emperor Hadrian intended the Wall as an answer to un-specified disturbances occurring in Britain in the early years of the second century AD; it consisted of a massive military fortification, built between 122 and 128, and stretched 117 km across northern England from the river Tyne to the Solway Firth. North of the Wall is a V-shaped ditch and south of it a flat-bottomed ditch traditionally known as the *Vallum*. At every Roman mile along the structure was a milecastle, and between each pair of milecastles were two turrets. There were also sixteen forts on or near the Wall, and outpost forts to the north. As first conceived, the eastern part of the Wall, from Newcastle to the river Irthing, was to be constructed of stone; the western stretch, to Bowness, was to be of turf. The stone wall was originally intended to be 3 metres wide, but much of it is only 2.4 metres on 3 metre foundations. The original turf wall was later replaced by a 2.7 metre wide stone wall, completed by 163. The Wall stood perhaps 6.1 metres high, with a 1.8 metres parapet.

The ditch averaged 8.2 metres across and 2.7 metres in depth. The Vallum ditch was 6.1 metres wide and 3 metres deep, its flat bottom about 2.4 metres wide. The material excavated from this ditch was piled in two continuous banks 9.1 metres back from either side of the ditch. This bank and ditch system could be crossed only by causeways at certain selected points and formed in effect the rearward part of the frontier line of Roman Britain.

The milecastles provided accommodation for the auxiliary troops patrolling the Wall. They were constructed first and the Wall was then built up to them. They were all based on a uniform plan but with slight internal differences. They held up to fifty men, usually in two barracks on either side of the road running through the centre of the structure. From the beginning of the third century the large milecastle gates giving access to the north (enabling the garrisons to launch attacks on enemy raiders) were part-blocked to postern size. The original turf-wall milecastles were of a similar pattern to the stone ones but were of turf and timber.

The two turrets between each pair of milecastles each covered an area of 1.9 square metres. They had two storeys, the upper one probably reached by a retractable ladder. Some two thousand men were required to patrol the Wall and man its buildings; they were quartered in the milecastles.

To give added support to the Wall's garrison, sixteen forts were built along the Wall line, each holding five hundred to a thousand men. There were also three outpost forts ahead of the Wall, and a system of forts, fortlets and watchtowers extended the defences for a further 65 km along the coast of Cumbria. A number of the

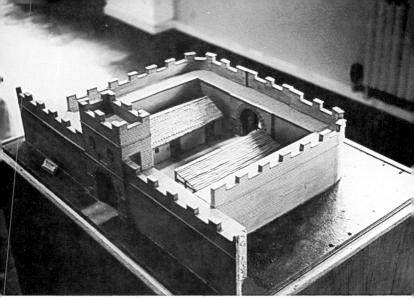

18. Hadrian's Wall: model of a typical milecastle in the Museum of Antiquities, the University, Newcastle upon Tyne.

19. Hadrian's Wall: model of a typical wall-fort in the Museum of Antiquities, the University, Newcastle upon Tyne.

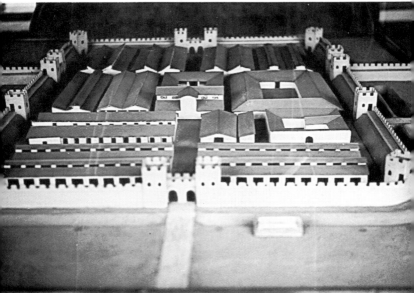

Wall forts have been partly excavated and are open for inspection. Though varying in size, they are more or less uniform in layout. Each presumably had its large extramural *vicus*, for here were born and brought up the succeeding generations of garrison troops; the Wall was manned by Britons, not by Romans. Outside the walls were the bath-houses for the troops and also small temples, such as the one at Carrawburgh (below, 11) to Mithras, a god popular with the Roman army.

With the building of the Antonine Wall (142) Hadrian's Wall lost its strategic importance, but by 164 the former had been abandoned and the frontier was again established on the Tyne-Solway line. In 196-7 the Wall was severely damaged during Pictish incursions and was later substantially repaired. A long period of peace followed, broken in 296 when the usurper Allectus withdrew the Wall garrison in an effort to claim the imperial throne. Once more the northern invaders caused serious damage to the Wall, which in turn was made good by 306. The last great barbarian invasion occurred in 367 when a combined force of Picts, Scots and Saxons overwhelmed the Wall and drove south, burning and pillaging as they went. In 369 the Wall was again denuded of its troops for another attempt at seizing the Empire. The soldiers never returned and the Wall was eventually left to the control of native troops and was virtually abandoned as a defence line.

Hadrian's Wall is the greatest Roman military work that still

20. Hadrian's Wall, looking east from Housesteads fort.

survives partly intact. Fortunately, large stretches have been preserved and are open to view. Only by a visit can one really appreciate its rugged grandeur as it rises and falls impressively over the highest points of the landscape of northern England.

1. Wallsend *Sedgedunum*: fort   SZ 305665

Take the A187 from Newcastle to Wallsend and the Tyne Tunnel. The site is just beyond Buddle Industrial Estate.

Wallsend marks the eastern end of Hadrian's Wall, which was extended in *c*.124 to the coast for security. The fort was occupied in the third and fourth centuries by a part infantry, part cavalry cohort of Lingones. The site of the fort has long been known beneath nineteenth-century housing, and excavations began in 1975 in advance of redevelopment. Part of the site is again beneath houses, the rest has been grassed and the outlines marked out. Some masonry of the east gate is preserved, and the *principia* conserved. A visit to the site should include the Wallsend Heritage Centre across the road from the east gate.

2. Benwell: temple and Vallum crossing   NZ 217646 and 215646

Both sites are just south of the A69 at Benwell. The temple, on Broomridge Avenue, is signposted by English Heritage. The Vallum crossing is at the bottom of Denhill Park Avenue.

21. Benwell, Hadrian's Wall: the tiny temple of Antenociticus.

The diminutive temple of Antenociticus, only 4.9 by 3 metres internally, lay outside the now built-over fort of *Condercum* on its east side, but inside the Vallum. In the apse at its southern end stood the statue of the god, flanked by altars dedicated by commanders of the garrison. The head of the statue and the altars are in the Museum of Antiquities at the University of Newcastle upon Tyne.

Opposite the south gate of the fort a section of the Vallum ditch was left undug, forming a natural causeway whose vertical sides were revetted in masonry. In the centre of the causeway stood a well-built gateway whose heavy doors were opened from the north. The metalling of the roadway was renewed at least once and new pivot holes were also provided for the doors. This type of crossing was provided at every fort on the Wall for controlled frontier access in the Hadrianic scheme, but the one at Benwell is the only one still visible. The effectiveness of the Vallum as a barrier can be appreciated by viewing the ditch sectors cleared out on either side of the causeway.

3. Denton: Turret 7b and Wall   NZ 198655
Alongside the A69(T) at Denton, west of Newcastle.

The turret, excavated in 1929, measures 4 by 4.2 metres internally and is recessed 1.5 metres into the Wall. It contains its ladder platform giving access to the first storey. The adjacent lengths of Wall are from three to five courses high, and some of the masonry in the lowest course is very massive.

4. Heddon on the Wall   NZ 137669
In a field south of the A69 and immediately east of the village.

This length of Wall measures 101 metres. It is 2.9 metres thick on a flagstone foundation 3.2 metres wide. The north face is four courses high, the south seven. The stones are now set in mortar to preserve them; originally they were set in puddled clay.

5. Corbridge *Coriosopitum* (?): supply base NY 982658
Take the minor road leading west from Corbridge, which is signposted by English Heritage.

The original fort was built by Agricola and was thereafter a base for the successive campaigns in the north. With the building of Hadrian's Wall the fort was abandoned but was reoccupied about 139 and drastically remodelled shortly after 161. For Severus' northern campaigns in the early third century Corbridge was made a supply base, and subsequently part of the site became a military arsenal for the manufacture of weapons and other objects for the army. At the same time a flourishing town grew up around it. Both arsenal and town were damaged in the troubles after 296. They were rebuilt, only to suffer again in 367.

22. Hadrian's Wall: model of Vallum and gateway in the Museum of Antiquities, the University, Newcastle upon Tyne.

The buildings on view belong mostly to the Severan phase and later. The main street shows the fourth-century surface, which is several feet higher than the two well preserved granaries to the north. This is the Stanegate passing through the fort. Beside it, the cistern with the scalloped sides (the result of centuries of knife sharpening) is the end of an aqueduct that supplied the fort from the north. Beyond this, on the same side of the street, are the lowest courses of an unfinished storehouse of the second century: note how the blocks were cut to fit at the edges and how the rusticated surface was left to be smoothed off later. To the south are the two compounds of the arsenal, each with its own workshops and administrative buildings, later united in a single enclosure in the post-296 reconstruction. Outside the compound walls are the shrines of the deities worshipped by the men, known from altars and dedications now in the site museum. This museum also contains the famous Corbridge Lion, devouring a stag; it was part of a tombstone adapted as the coping of a water tank in a domestic building, the lion's mouth carrying a water pipe.

6. Brunton: Turret 28b and Wall   NY 921699
Turn off the B6318 at Low Brunton, on to the A6079. The site is signposted a short distance on the left.
   This turret, 3.9 by 3.5 metres internally, is embodied in a length of wall still 2.6 metres high. It is in a fine state of preservation.

23. *Corbridge, Hadrian's Wall: the aqueduct.*

7. Chesters: bridge abutment   NY 914700

This is a separate visit from Chesters fort, as it is on the opposite side of the river. Take the path that starts alongside the B6318 (signposted) and runs along the disused railway line.

When the North Tyne is low, two piers of this bridge can be seen in the water. A third lies embedded in the east bank. The eastern abutment was exposed in 1860. Here the Wall, 1.9 metres thick on the broad foundation, ended in a tower 6.7 metres square.

Enclosed in the abutment is a smaller pier with two cutwaters, belonging to an earlier bridge which originally carried the Wall on a series of stone arches, later replaced in timber. The abutment tower guarded the bridge and housed a mill, powered by river water channelled through the abutment in a millrace — as at Willowford (below, 19). Keen eyes might spot the phallus (a good luck symbol) carved on a stone in the north face.

8. Chesters *Cilurnum*: fort and bath-house   NY 912701

The entrance is south of the B6318 and is signposted.

The fort, originally built for a cavalry regiment, was occupied by an infantry cohort and in turn by a cavalry unit in the third

24. Chesters, Hadrian's Wall: the military bath-house.

century. The front third of the fort projects beyond the Wall, which abuts on the south towers of the east and west gates. The Wall, which is thus later in construction than the fort, is of narrow gauge, standing on the broad foundation. This foundation runs beneath the fort, and in 1945 the demolished remains of Turret 27a were found east of the *principia*. This construction shows the fort to be a secondary feature but added at an early stage before the Wall itself had been erected.

The fort's gates and the south angle and interval towers are open for inspection, as are many of the internal buildings. Especially noteworthy here is the *principia* with a basement strong-room; also visible are the foundations of parts of three barrack blocks and the commandant's house and baths.

East of the fort and close by the river is the fort's bath-house, an elaborate establishment with a large changing room, four heated rooms in the main suite and a separately stoked *laconicum*. The hot tank was over the hypocaust flue of the *caldarium*, from which the hot water was piped round to the hot bath (note the remains of the narrow window, which was originally glazed), while the overflow from the cold tank was used to flush the latrines before passing out to the river.

The Clayton Memorial Museum on the site contains a fine collection of objects from the fort and other sites on the Wall.

9. Black Carts: Turret 29a and Wall   NY 884713

The turret is visible to the north from the B6318. Access is via a minor road to the north.

The remains include a good stretch of Wall, 1.8 metres high and overshadowed by trees. In this stretch are the remains of Turret 29a, cleared in 1873. It measures internally 3.6 by 3.5 metres and has wing walls of broad gauge. Its door jambs are of single large stones. At its highest point the turret has fourteen courses.

10. Limestone Corner: unfinished ditch   NY 876716

Park in the lay-by on the north side of the B6318. A nearby iron gate leads to the site.

The remains here consist of a stretch of ditch left unfinished, possibly because of the hardness of the underlying rock. Some of the holes in the quarried blocks were intended for wedges, others for lewis blocks on the enormous cranes that would have been necessary.

11. Carrawburgh *Brocolitia*: fort and Mithraeum
NY 858712

The fort is beside the B6318 to the south. A car park is provided.

Little of the fort is visible except for the grassed-over remains of the unexcavated walls. The fort was a late addition to the original scheme and was built over the Vallum, which had already been constructed.

The Mithraeum is south-west of the fort and was discovered when ground shrinkage during the drought of 1949 revealed the tops of three altars still *in situ*. The rectangular building, dedicated to the cult of Mithras, was built soon after 205, enlarged to twice its original size and twice refurbished during the third century. It was destroyed by the Picts in 297 and completely rebuilt before its deliberate desecration, presumably on the orders of a Christian commandant. The altars and other features (including the wattlework of the benches) have been reproduced in concrete on the site; an excellent life-sized reproduction (somewhat foreshortened recently) of the Mithraeum during its period of use, with recorded commentary, can be seen in the Museum of Antiquities in the University of Newcastle upon Tyne.

To the west of the fort, within a fence, is the famous Coventina's Well, which produced in 1876 a great mass of coins, jewellery, votive objects and carved stones.

25. Carrawburgh, Hadrian's Wall: three water-nymphs from Coventina's well.

12. Housesteads *Vercovicium*: fort, Wall and Milecastle 37
NY 789687

The car park is signposted on the north side of the B6318. A five-minute walk brings one first to the site museum and then to the fort.

The fort covers about 2 hectares; it is laid out with its long axis along the line of the Wall and its main gate facing east. The arrangement is necessitated by the site, on the narrow shelf of the Whin Sill, between a steep slope to the south and precipitous cliffs to the north. Its garrison was an infantry cohort eight hundred strong, reinforced in the third century by cavalry and infantry.

It occupies the site of an earlier turret (36b), whose remains and those of the broad foundation were found just inside the north wall of the fort. The whole of the fort's interior has been excavated, and much is left on view. The *principia* and granaries are well preserved, as are the latrines in the south-east angle. Near the *principia* lies the hospital, the only example to be seen in Britain today. In the north-east corner a barrack block has been preserved in its late fourth-century state — a series of 'chalets', each with one or two rooms, for a militia that was very different from that of the second century.

Outside the south gate are the remains of three houses of an extensive *vicus*. Down the slope to the east, in the valley of the

Knag Burn, was a gateway in the Wall, with front and rear doors, for customs control under the supervision of the garrison. This gateway seems to have been inserted in the early fourth century.

West of the fort is a fine stretch of the Wall. The south face was restored in the nineteenth century and more recently, although the north face is still in disrepair. The width of the Wall here varies slightly in places because different centuries worked simultaneously on different parts of the line.

This part of the Wall contains Milecastle 37, an excellent example of its kind. It measures internally 15 metres (north to south) by 18 metres (east to west). The side walls are 2.7 metres thick and the gates are of massive masonry, with arches at the front and back. The north gate was narrowed to a postern in the time of Severus. The western half of the milecastle was occupied by a timber stores shed, the eastern by a two-roomed barrack block, the foundations of which still remain.

13. Chesterholm *Vindolanda*: fort and vicus   NY 770664

Take the minor road south off the B6318 at Twice Brewed. The site is well signposted from this point. There is a large car park.

The fort was founded by Agricola as part of the Stanegate system, abandoned under Hadrian when the garrison was moved up to the Wall and reoccupied about 163. Under Severus and Caracalla a new fort was laid out on the site, facing south. This was completely rebuilt by Constantius I, who turned it to face north, and it was extensively repaired in 369.

The visible remains, covering 1.4 hectares, date to Constantius' reconstruction. At the eastern gate the Severan masonry has been incorporated into the later work, and traces of the Severan headquarters have been detected below the fine *principia* of Constantius. Noteworthy features of the latter include the tribunal and stone screens in the cross-hall, and the pit for the regimental pay chests. In the later fourth century these headquarters became living accommodation and storehouses.

Also visible are the north and west gates and the west and east walls.

To the west is a considerable civilian settlement (which originally served the Hadrianic fort), under excavation for a number of years by Robin Birley and the Vindolanda Trust. With much voluntary labour, this body has uncovered many of the foundations of the numerous buildings of this *vicus*, including a *mansio* and an extensive bath-house fed by a stone conduit. The fragmentary leaves of a large number of writing tablets (*c.* AD 80-125) have been discovered and have proved perhaps the most important of all the discoveries at Vindolanda.

26. Chesterholm (Vindolanda), Hadrian's Wall: a milestone beside the Stanegate.

Reconstructions of sections of both stone and turf stretches of Hadrian's Wall, with associated turrets, can be seen at the site, and the adjoining house, Chesterholm, now houses the headquarters of the Trust and a fine museum.

Also noteworthy is a milestone, a fine column 1.8 metres high, standing in its original position beside the Stanegate, north of the farm.

14. Castle Nick: Milecastle 39 and Wall   NY 760676
Take the minor road off the B6318 at 753669 to Steel Rigg car park, to the north. The line of the Wall can be seen to the east. Walk along the Wall to the site. Milecastle 40 (below, 15) lies to the west.

The shell of this milecastle measures 15 metres east to west by 19 metres north to south. Its gateways are constructed of small masonry. Its walls are 2.1 metres thick and stand six or seven courses high. The foundations of a small barrack block can be seen on the west side.

15. Winshiels: Milecastle 40 and Wall   NY 745666
See directions for Castle Nick (above, 14).

This area includes the highest point on the whole Wall, 375 metres above sea level. The milecastle has walls 2.1 metres thick and gateways (like those of Milecastle 39) in small masonry more easily transported to these two remote sites. West of the milecastle the wall is in a good state of preservation. English Heritage has grouted the wall core and reset the facing stones.

16. Cawfields: Milecastle 42   NY 716667
Turn north off the B6318 at 716660; the site is reached by a track to the east of the road.

When visiting the site note the earthworks of Haltwhistle Burn fort on the hillock immediately east of the burn, close to the road. The fort, 63 by 51 metres, is one of the small forts in the first scheme for the Wall. Note, too, a temporary Roman camp to the east of the track to the milecastle, and a fine view of the Vallum coming from the west. The milecastle measures 19 metres east to west by 15 metres north to south. Its walls stand seven or eight courses high and are 2.4 metres thick. Both gates are of massive masonry and the south gate stands high enough to display the bolt hole for fastening the door.

17. Greatchesters *Aesica*: fort   NY 704667
Take the minor road north from the B6318. A footpath leads west to the fort at 712666.

Aesica was built late in the sequence of Wall building about 128, when the broad wall and Milecastle 43 had already been constructed, and — like Carrawburgh (above, 11) — lies wholly to the south of the Wall line. The fort measures 128 by 102 metres but is much overgrown and neglected. The best feature is the west gate, which was at some late stage completely blocked and still retains the blocking walls in position. This is unusual, since early excavators usually removed blocking walls to expose original masonry, leaving no complete record of the features. Knowledge of the internal buildings is fragmentary, but a bathhouse was found 91 metres south of the fort. The site received its water via an aqueduct, consisting of a 0.9-1.2 metres deep channel running from the head of Haltwhistle Burn for a winding length of 10 km.

18. Carvoran *Banna* or *Magna*: museum   NY 665657
Take a minor road north from the B6318 at 668655 to Carvoran house, where the Roman Army Museum is signposted.

This museum was opened in 1981 in converted farm buildings adjoining the house, as a private venture. The displays, consisting of reconstructions, models and audio-visual presentations are dedicated to the Roman soldier and his way of life in the context of Roman Britain and particularly Hadrian's Wall. Of the fort nearby only the north rampart can now be seen.

19. Willowford: Turrets 48a and b, Wall and bridge

NY 622665

The sites are west of a minor road leading south-west from Gilsland.

An excellent stretch of Hadrian's Wall about 800 metres long can be followed, running from just west of the road down to the bridge abutment by the river Irthing. The Wall stands up to fourteen courses high and is here 8 Roman feet across (i.e. the narrow-gauge thickness raised on the broad wall foundations, forming a wide shallow 'step' alongside the Wall). Set in the structure are the remains of Turrets 48a and b.

Willowford bridge was rebuilt at least once during Roman times. Originally it had massive segmental arches to carry the weight of the Wall and the splayed foundation of its abutment is embedded in the later work. A turret once stood on this abutment, but this was dismantled during the reconstruction. It its place a large tower was positioned a little to the east. One of the three piers can be seen to the west of the enlarged abutment, the stream bed in between being paved to form an emplacement for a mill wheel. The other piers lie beneath the riverbank in the original gorge of the Irthing, from which the river was probably diverted west by the choking of the bridge itself.

20. Birdoswald *Camboglanna*: fort and Wall   NY 615663

Take the B6318 west of Greenhead. Turn south along a minor road signposted 'Lanercost Priory and Turret 49b'. This road passes the fort.

Camboglanna was originally designed for a cavalry garrison but was occupied by an infantry cohort eight hundred strong. It was built on the site of the Turf Wall, which can be seen as a low bump running through the field to the east. The stone wall which replaced it took a more northerly course to join the north angles of the fort, leaving the east and west gates behind the revised line. The fort walls, main south and east gates, west postern and some interval towers can be seen. West of the fort is a good stretch of the Wall, 2.3 metres thick on a 2.4 metres wide foundation. This sector of the Wall includes Turret 49b. East of the fort is another well conserved stretch of the Wall leading to Milecastle 49. The visible remains of this stand on the site of an earlier Turf Wall milecastle. The milecastle is 23 metres north to south and 20 metres east to west and stands seven courses high on the south side.

27. Birdoswald, Hadrian's Wall: the east gate.

21. Appletree: Turf Wall NY 597655
Take a minor road west from Birdoswald. Turn right down the lane at Appletree — a former cottage now turned into a barn. The site is 45 metres down the lane.

A section has been cut through the Turf Wall here which shows the laminated structure of the rampart in alternate blocks of whitish bleached roots, humus and streaks of dark carbonised grass.

22. Coombe Crag: Roman quarry and inscriptions
NY 591650
Take a minor road west from Birdoswald. West of Wall Bowers is a lodge on the left of the road, from which a path leads to Coombe Crag quarry.

The quarry was extensively worked by the Romans, who left a number of visible inscriptions on the rock faces. Among them can be seen *SECVRVS*, *IVSTVS* and *MATERNVS*. At the foot of the cliff is a spurious inscription, *FAVST ET RVF COS*, recognisable by the freshness of the cutting and the difference in the style of inscription.

23. Banks East: Turret 52a and Wall NY 575647
The turret is just south of the minor road leading east from Banks village.

Originally a Turf Wall structure, the masonry turret has a plinth at the front and rear and still stands fourteen courses high. Adjoining the turret is a well-preserved piece of the Wall.

24. Banks Burn: Wall   NY 562646(E)

The site is immediately to the west of Banks village.

A fine stretch of the Wall is visible west of the site of Milecastle 53. The Wall stands 3 metres high but was refaced in the nineteenth century. In its north face a centurial stone, found nearby at Moneyholes, records the century of a *primus pilus* (chief centurion).

25. Maryport *Alauna*: fort   NY 038373

The site is north of the modern town, at the end of Camp Street.

The remains of this 2.3 hectares fort overlook the Irish Sea. The position of the four gates can still be seen. To the south of the fort was a levelled parade ground with an adjacent tribunal where a remarkable series of altars was found in 1870, buried in pits. An extensive civil settlement lay outside the fort to the north, and excavations have revealed the foundations of houses, shops, taverns, etc.

26. Ravenglass *Glannaventa*: fort and bath-house

SD 087961

The fort is beside the railway line south-west of Ravenglass, accessible via a track leading south from the minor road at 087966.

The site of this 1.6 hectares fort has been cut through by the railway. It stands on the edge of the harbour just south of Ravenglass, bounded on the west by cliffs and on the south and north by the Mite and Esk valleys. Although little can be seen of

28. Hadrian's Wall: an inscription by a vexillation of the Twentieth Legion Valeria Victrix, flanked by a centurion and Hercules.

the fort its bath-house (called Walls Castle locally) is well preserved. The walls are built of coursed red freestone and stand almost 4 metres high. Two doorways can be seen, and traces of five splayed windows. The wall of one room, perhaps the entrance hall, contains a round-headed niche.

HAMPSHIRE

1. Alice Holt Forest: kiln sites   SU 808403
The sites are 6 km south of Farnham on the A325. The Forest Information Service is at Bucks Horn Oak (808417).

Excavation and research have shown that pottery was made in the area from early in the Roman occupation until the beginning of the fifth century AD. The Alice Holt Forest is on gault clay and provided the necessary raw materials except sand, which was available from the neighbouring heathlands. The kilns produced both large storage vessels and smaller everyday items such as flagons. These products were transported over large distances to London, Kent, Surrey and further afield into Essex and Gloucestershire.

There are waste dumps in the forest on both sides of the A325, with the main concentration in the southern part of the forest. Over 82 dumps have been recognised by work carried out since 1971 by the Alice Holt Survey Group. A kiln excavated in 1977 confirmed earlier findings that kilns in the area were of the double flue variety, with several rebuildings overlying one another. To confirm the results of this dig, an experimental kiln was built and fired in the Goose Green enclosure in 1977.

To view the pottery dumps it is best to visit in the winter when the leaf cover is at its lowest. Pottery is still made today at nearby Wrecclesham (825446).

2. Bitterne *Clausentum*(?): fort   SU 434134
Take the Portsmouth road out of Southampton, cross Northam Bridge and park by Bitterne railway station (438134). Walk back along the main road to the first of the two entrances, which gives access to the site, now a small park.

The promontory created by a bend in the river Itchen was cut in antiquity by two lines of defences. The outer, now approximately represented by Rampart Road, was conceivably iron age in date, but in its final Roman form apparently enclosed a small settlement. A minor road from the east entered the promontory and ran to its western tip, where there seems to have been a small port in the late first century. Excavation has dated the development of the settlement to the later fourth century, when the inner defences were built. An inner ditch and wall, possibly with a bank and reportedly with terminal towers and a towered gateway, cut the promontory, the wall being extended around it to form a D-shaped fort or walled town. Occupation probably continued between this and the outer defences. This structure is often thought of as part of the Saxon Shore defences, possibly even a replacement for Portchester, whose harbour may have been silting up.

Today, only a much enlarged section of the Inner Fosse is visible as an overgrown cavity among the trees; the wall is visible only on private land by the foreshore. A tiny bath-house has been conserved at the north-west corner of the Manor but is now strictly out of bounds to visitors. A four-roomed suite of *c.*175, it was converted subsequently into a two-roomed dwelling. A further conversion into baths again in *c.*370 was left unfinished.

The Burghal Hidage document suggests reoccupation of the walled area as a *burh* under Alfred.

Faint traces of the approach road across Peartree Common are marked by a plaque at 447127.

3. Bokerly Dyke: boundary dyke and road   SU 035200

The A354 cuts through this earthwork at a point 14 km south-west of Salisbury where the road bends and takes on the alignment of the Roman road, Ackling Dyke. Park in the lay-by at the bend.

This earthwork forms the boundary between Hampshire and Dorset and was constructed in about 325-30 to protect the downland settlements of north-east Dorset against marauders from the north, across a 6 km neck of land flanked by forests. To the east of the lay-by the great bank and ditch appear to be a

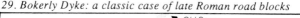

29. *Bokerly Dyke: a classic case of late Roman road blocks*

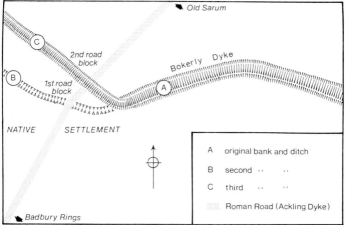

simple earthwork; it is in fact of two main phases, and to the west of the lay-by it has two extensions. The southernmost, the Rear Dyke, was demolished in Roman times, when the more northerly Fore Dyke replaced it. Before looking for this, note the fine *agger* of the Roman road, the Ackling Dyke, as it approaches from the north.

The story has been reconstructed from excavation. Initially, the road passed by the barrier; before long, however, the Rear Dyke was built across the road, to block it, and the occasion was probably the period of crisis in 367 that frightened the entire province. The crisis passed, and the road was reopened a few years later. Finally, in the last years of the Roman occupation, probably some time after 395, the earthworks were rebuilt on a more forward line (the Fore Dyke) and the road was blocked once more. This time it was not reopened.

The road is in superb condition as it leads southwards to Badbury Rings. For this section see Ackling Dyke (Dorset, 1).

4. Farley Mount: road   SU 452291-410295
Leave Winchester by the Romsey road, A3090; after 1.6 km, where the road forks left, go straight ahead along Sarum Road, a leafy minor road. The Farley Mount picnic area is 3 km further on.

This section of the Roman road from Winchester to Old Sarum can be followed for just under 3 km by car. On the south edge of Crab Wood the modern road is on the *agger* and a pronounced side ditch can be seen on the north side. At 423294 the modern road bends left while the Roman road goes straight ahead. It can be walked for a distance of about 1.6 km, passing south of the site of the Sparsholt villa (SU 415301), where nothing can be seen at present. Plans, however, are in hand to mark the site for visitors with explanatory signs. A fine geometric mosaic and some noteworthy wall plaster from the villa can be seen in Winchester City Museum.

5. Portchester *Portus Adurni*   SU 625045
On the tip of the promontory 1.2 km south of Portchester and south of the A27 at the head of Portsmouth Harbour. Guidebook available.

This fort is mentioned in the *Notitia* and is one of the finest and the most western of the Saxon Shore forts. Unlike Pevensey, its neighbour, the sea still reaches up to the fort as it did in Roman times. The plan is basically Roman with medieval refacing to the walls, which are 3 metres thick and stand to a height of 5.5 metres. It encloses an area of 3.6 hectares, and originally there were two main gates, east and west, and two posterns. Of the

30. Portchester, Hampshire.

west gate only the foundations can be seen, the present gatehouse being a narrower medieval insertion. The Watergate is entirely Saxon and medieval, and the posterns to north and south are blocked. Around the outside of the walls there were originally twenty bastions; fourteen remain today. They are all hollow, unlike those at other forts in the series, which are solid. At the north-west corner there is a fine Norman keep and associated castle. In the south-east corner is the twelfth-century church of St Mary. Excavations have shown that the fort was evacuated in 296 after the Carausian episode, recommissioned in *c.*340 for about thirty years with a regular garrison before being handed to a non-Roman mercenary garrison of Germanic character. Anglo-Saxon farming and occupation within the walls continued up to the Norman Conquest.

6. Portway: road

SU 463523-502543

The Roman road is a byroad crossing the B3051, 3 km south of Kingsclere.

This is a section of the road from Old Sarum to Silchester, the whole route covering a distance of 58 km. Portions of the route are completely under the plough, whilst others have modern metalling.

The portion stretching from a point west of Hannington to Clap Gate starts as a modern road; after crossing the B3051, it becomes a track for 275 metres, then a modern road to Caesar's Belt, a line of 5 km of trees and shrubs. This can be walked, the path being on the north side of the Belt.

7. Rockbourne: villa

SU 120170

The villa is in West Park, 5 km north-west of Fordingbridge, on the south side of a minor road to Rockbourne. Leave Fordingbridge by the B3078 in the direction of Cranborne and turn right after 2.5 km. A guidebook is available.

This private site, which was kept open during excavations from 1956 to 1976 and attracted many thousands of visitors, is now in the care of Hampshire County Council, which has backfilled and grassed it to prevent further deterioration. Parts, however, including mosaics and a hypocaust of unusual form, using paired *imbrices* in place of the usual *pilae*, are now conserved for display, while the remainder is now marked out on the site. The former site museum is now a display area; its contents are mostly stored in Winchester.

In the centre of the site a simple masonry strip building of the first century AD had been built over an earlier circular iron age hut. It was superseded by a larger establishment in the second century. By the fourth this had developed into a large courtyard villa enclosed on at least three sides. The main residential wing lay to the north-west, with a large bath suite to the south and farm buildings occupying the rest.

8. Silchester *Calleva Atrebatum*

SU 640625

The site is in open country,16 km south of Reading and 10 km north of Basingstoke, via side roads 3 km north-east of the A340. Park by the church. There is a small site museum west of the town area, near the Rectory at the end of The Drove. A tour of the site should be accompanied by a visit to Reading Museum, which is closed at the time of writing but due to reopen in the mid 1990s. Material in store is available for study by prior arrangement with the museum. A guidebook can be obtained at the site museum.

The deserted Roman town, the capital of the *civitas* of the Atrebates, covers 43 hectares and stands on the site of a Belgic

31. Rockbourne, Hampshire: the unusual hypocaust.

settlement occupied in the first century BC. By the time of the Roman conquest it had come under the domination of the Catuvellauni. The present shape of the town is polygonal, and although it had a regular street plan by about AD 90-120 it is clear

32. Rockbourne, Hampshire: mosaic.

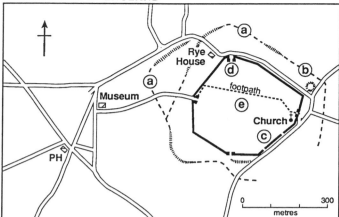

33. *Plan of Silchester showing sites described in the text: a, first defensive circuit; b, amphitheatre; c, south wall; d, north gate; e, possible church.*

that the first defensive circuit (marked by the outer earthwork) (a) was too large and never fully built up. Realism prevailed by the end of the second century and the final outline was much reduced — a bank and ditch to which the existing stone wall was added later in the third century. The town when complete had four main gates and three postern gates. One of these on the north-east gave access to the amphitheatre (b) outside the walls. This has recently been excavated and conserved and is well worth a visit. *Calleva* was served by seven roads from London, Gloucester, Alchester, Old Sarum, Winchester, St Albans and Chichester. Long stretches of the walls can be seen from Wall Lane on the north and Church Lane on the south; a walk along the newly restored south wall (c) is especially rewarding. Further conservation is in progress on the north wall, and the north gate (d) can be visited on application to Rye House in Wall Lane.

Much of the interior was superficially excavated between 1890 and 1909 but wholly backfilled. The plan of the town thus recovered includes only buildings with stone foundations. The town had a bath-house, three square temples and one octagonal one. An unusual feature was a small apsidal building near the forum (e), generally interpreted as a church. The town was abandoned after the Roman period. In the north-west corner an ogham inscription, cut on a reused column drum, was found in a well. It commemorates an Irish mercenary soldier or pilgrim and is the most easterly known ogham monument. It is held by Reading Museum with most of the other finds, which include a large selection of woodworking tools. In the churchyard is a small column from one of the two temples which lie beneath.

9. Winchester *Venta Belgarum*   SU 482295 (centre)

The visitor in search of Roman Winchester is likely to be disappointed, though the medieval and post-medieval city has much to offer.

Venta was adopted as the capital city of the Roman *civitas* of the Belgae, and at its height was — at 58 hectares — the fifth largest in Roman Britain. The strength of its pre-Roman predecessor can be gauged from the much reduced earthworks preserved just outside the Roman defences at Oram's Arbour (475297) (a). Excavation has shown that the first defences (*c*. AD 70) were of earth and timber and that the street grid was laid out some twenty years later. By the end of the first century the *forum* was created (to the north of the cathedral) with other public buildings in brick and stone. In succeeding centuries the simple timber houses were replaced by more elaborate town-houses with mosaics and wall plaster. Examples of these last can be seen in the City Museum in The Square (near the cathedral) and the site of one house is marked in St George's Street (b). Substantial cemeteries developed at the city gates. The Roman city wall was replaced on

34. Plan of Winchester showing the sites described in the text: a, Oram's Arbour; b, St George's Street; c, Roman city wall; d, Castle; e, Roman milestone; f, Deanery; g, mosaic.

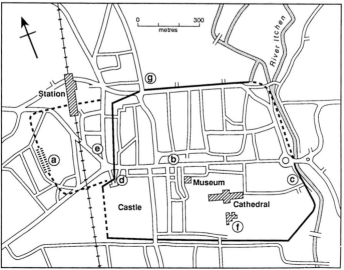

the north and west sides by the medieval defences, much of which can be traced. A footpath running south from the Mill, 140 metres east of King Alfred's statue, follows the walls, and part of the Roman masonry is visible behind a grating (c); a further piece is displayed between the medieval West Gate and the Great Hall of the castle (in which the Round Table is on show) (d). Here can also be seen the medieval wall with a bastion and sallyport of the castle. Just to the north of the West Gate an uninscribed cylindrical stone built into the wall by the shops opposite the former barracks is believed to be a Roman milestone (e); it is certainly beside the line of the Roman road to Old Sarum (Hampshire, 4). A further mosaic fragment has been relaid in the porch of the Deanery, in the Cathedral Close, and can be examined with permission (f). The City Museum covers the Winchester district, while excavation records and materials can be consulted at the Historic Resources Centre in Hyde Street. Here, on public display under an archway, is a black and white Roman mosaic of unknown provenance but of Italian workmanship and doubtless a recent souvenir of the grand tour rather than a relic of Roman Winchester (g).

HEREFORD AND WORCESTER

1. Kenchester *Magnis*: town   SO 440428
The site is in fields to the north of a minor road, 1.6 km south-west of Kenchester.

Little that is visible remains of the Roman town. The site is represented by a hexagonal bank enclosing 8.9 hectares. It was defended by a stone wall 2.1 metres thick, perhaps backed by an earthen bank. Although an eighteenth-century plan shows four gateways, none is now visible above ground. Sporadic excavations have revealed the general layout of the town, but no definite date has yet been assigned to it. Excavators have uncovered paved streets, drainage channels and house foundations with mosaic floors and decorated wall plaster. Inhumation and cremation burials have been found *within* the walls and a variety of small finds, including pottery and coins, have been made. The town was perhaps founded during the second half of the first century AD and abandoned some time in the fourth.

HERTFORDSHIRE

1. Harpenden: mausoleum   TL 119136
The site is in the private grounds of the Rothamstead Experimental Station.

The circular stone building, 3.4 metres in diameter, stood in an enclosure about 30 metres square, surrounded by a wall with an entrance in its eastern face and an external V-shaped ditch. The circular foundations and part of the enclosure wall are displayed. The mausoleum may have been about 6.1 metres high; it contained an altar-like base set in front of an alcove that probably held a life-sized statue. Pieces of such a statue were found during excavation in 1937. Inside the square enclosure two cremation burials were found dating from about 130. It is probable that there were other tombs nearby.

2. St Albans *Verulamium*   Museum at TL 136073

The fine museum is a good starting point for all visits to Verulamium. There is a large car park behind it.

The Catuvellauni, a Belgic tribe, had their capital at or near Prae Wood (TL 126070), 2 km due west of St Albans Abbey. The site, consisting of numerous low banks and ditches, is extremely overgrown and on private land. The earthworks surrounding *Verulamium* are very extensive but hard to trace; Beech Bottom Dyke, however, is a good specimen and can be found in the outskirts of the city, beside Beech Road.

The earliest Roman town lay north of St Michael's church, between Prae Wood and the river Ver. Little is known about it,

35. Plan of St Albans showing the sites described in the text: a, basilica and forum; b, Roman theatre; c, hypocaust; d, Roman wall; e, London Gate.

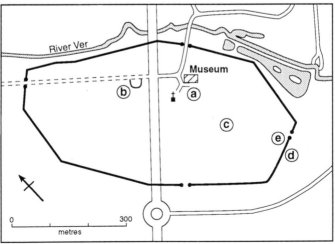

save that it was destroyed by Boudicca in AD 60. The town took twenty years to rebuild, the *basilica* being completed in AD 79. It was defended by an earth and timber rampart and ditch, which can still be seen on the north-west side of the Roman town and is known as The Fosse (visible from close to Gorhambury Drive at TL 128077). *Verulamium* became the most important town in Roman Britain, with the status of *municipium*.

About 200 the Roman town was enclosed within a flint and tile wall and a massive ditch 9.1 metres wide and 6.1 metres deep. Inside the town were houses, shops and temples, though little of these can be seen today (see **b** and **c** below). Considering that hardly any of the Roman site is built upon, there is surprisingly little to be seen. St Albans clearly does not realise its tourist potential. To compensate, perhaps, the recently enlarged and redesigned museum displays the results of the excavations to good effect.

The best surviving remains are as follows:

a. The basilica and forum. The town hall and market place lie under St Michael's church. The corner of the *basilica* has been marked out in the grass on the west side of the museum near the car park.

b. The Roman theatre (TL 134074) lies north-west of the museum and across the A4147. The theatre is privately owned but open to the public. It had a chequered history with a number of rebuilds, being originally nearly circular in form — a native variety peculiar to Britain and part of Gaul. Rebuilt as a more orthodox Roman theatre, it was used for bear baiting and cock fighting as well as musical and dramatic performances. Since it was within the precinct of the nearby temple, performances of a religious nature must have predominated. Visitors should note that the high bank on which they walk is the dump of earth excavated from the theatre and not part of the structure. A detailed guidebook is available at the ticket office.

Beside the theatre can be seen wall footings of early houses and shops. The outlines marked in concrete show the plan of a parade of shops built of timber and destroyed by Boudicca some ten years after they were built. They fronted on to Watling Street, whose line is now marked approximately by Gorhambury Drive. Under one of the later masonry houses was a shrine. Although much of it was destroyed after excavation by the building of the A4147 the apse end of the shrine can still be seen.

c. The hypocaust (TL 136069). Under the park to the south of the museum lie the foundations of many fine buildings, but only

36. St Albans (Verulamium), Hertfordshire: the Roman theatre.

two rooms of one of these are visible to the public. It is protected by a modern brick bungalow and consists of a large mosaic pavement with a hypocaust underneath. Originally this was part of the bath wing of a great town-house 61 metres long and 40 metres wide, with a verandah and garden looking to the south-east. The mosaic was damaged by Norman monks from the Abbey who used the Roman ruins as a convenient quarry for bricks and tiles. This explains the attractive warm colouring and texture of the Abbey, whose tower is built almost entirely of Roman bricks.

d. Roman wall. A short section of wall can be seen close to the modern artificial lake (TL 139069). There was a Roman cemetery beneath this lake. The course of the wall can easily be seen running under the grass-covered banks, especially into the trees to the south-west of the lake at TL 136066. Here it often rises 3 metres high and is constructed of flint and layers of tiles. It is 3 metres wide at its base and must have risen to a height of about 7 metres. A path 4.6 metres wide separates the wall from the ditch, which has been excavated in recent years to its original depth of 6.1 metres. At intervals along the wall are solid semicircular bastions on which artillery was mounted and square internal towers used as stores, to house patrols and for observation.

37. *St Albans, Hertfordshire: the Roman walls.*

e. The London Gate (TL 13806⁷). This is situated at the point where the Watling Street entered the city on the southern side. It is marked in the grass with a flint outline. The two gates for vehicles and two passages for pedestrians can be seen flanked by guard chambers.

3. Welwyn: bath-house   TL 235158
Opposite the Clock Motel off the Old Welwyn bypass, a steel-lined tunnel leads under the A1(M) motorway. The site is open on Sunday and Bank Holiday afternoons or at other times by arrangement with the Mill Green Museum, telephone: 07072 71362.
   The Dicket Mead villa consisted of two long buildings 275 metres apart. These are no longer visible, except for the bath-house at the end of one of them, which lies under the motorway. Excavation has shown that the bath-house was constructed around 250 and consisted of three rooms, a *frigidarium*, *tepidarium* and *caldarium*, each about 2.4 metres square. Details of the villa are displayed on the walls around the remains.

HUMBERSIDE

1. Brough-on-Humber *Petuaria*: **town**   SE 937267
The site is east of the modern village.

Little of the Roman town of *Petuaria* is visible on the ground. The site began as a Flavian fort with a settlement on the south side. By the middle of the second century the fort had fallen out of use and *Petuaria* developed as a town and the *civitas* capital of the Parisii. The native huts were cleared and foundations begun for Roman-style buildings, though many were not completed until much later. The new town, defended by a turf rampart and a triple ditch, was large; it is possible that part of it was connected with a naval unit on the Humber.

The town was at its most prosperous during the second century, with a theatre probably associated with a temple. The defences were reorganised *c*.200 and a stone wall was added *c*.270. *Petuaria*'s importance had declined by the fourth century: this was probably caused by the silting of the harbour.

ISLE OF WIGHT

1. Brading: villa   SZ 599863
The villa is sited 800 metres south of Brading, off the A3055. There is a museum on the site, and a guidebook is available.

On pottery evidence this site was occupied in the first century AD, but the villa proper was built in the fourth century and occupied until the end of the Roman period. It is of the courtyard type, the main block being on the west side. Only the main building and parts of the north wing are now visible, the rest having been reburied. The north and south wings were presumably for labourers, animals and storage of crops. The water supply for the villa was a well 30 metres deep. The twelve rooms in the west wing have been roofed over and contain some fine mosaics. One shows Orpheus playing his lyre and surrounded by the animals he has pacified. The four seasons are illustrated in another mosaic, and in its side panel the story of Perseus and Andromeda is shown. There is a panel with an astrologer pointing with a rod towards a globe and in the eastern portion of the same room a fine head of Medusa with snakes entwined in her hair. In Room 1 note a T-shaped corn drier cut through the mosaic in the fourth century.

2. Brading Down: field system   SZ 595868
Brading Down lies to the south of a minor road towards Newport about 1.2 km west of Brading. The fields are best seen in the low light of evening or early morning.

This south-facing slope, just below the crest of the downs, can be seen from the Brading villa in the valley below; the fields seem to represent part of the arable and grazing land of the villa estate. By contrast with the sub-rectangular form of most 'Celtic' fields,

38. Brading, Isle of Wight: the mosaic with a cock-headed man.

this is a pattern of long fields, the result of ploughing with a heavier Roman plough that required fewer turns at the headland. In the north-west corner, beside the road, a bronze age barrow has been incorporated, and faint banks to the south of the road represent a pre-Roman earthwork, perhaps a hillfort, levelled by Roman cultivation.

3. Carisbrooke: fort   SZ 486877
Carisbrooke Castle is 1.6 km south-west of Newport and south of the B3401 on the road to Gatcombe.

The Norman and later castle stands on the site of what may have been a Roman fort. If so, it was the most westerly in the chain of Saxon Shore forts, and perhaps a late addition to the series. A portion of the Roman wall can be seen low down in the bank on the left-hand side as one crosses the bridge to enter the Great Gatehouse. This is known as the Lower Enclosure, and the masonry has been traced at intervals on all sides of the rectangular Norman earthwork. On the east side, part of a shallow bastion is seen exposed at the base of the motte. To the south of the bastion a portion of an inturned entrance, of late Roman form (as at Portchester, Hampshire, 5), can be seen; more of it was revealed by excavation beneath an adjacent medieval building.

The Roman date has often been questioned, since the copious pottery normal on Saxon Shore forts is notably lacking and the inland site is unusual. The distinctive stone, however, comes from the

Binstead facies of the local Bembridge limestone. This contrasts with the Quarr facies of the same stone which was almost exclusively favoured by Saxon builders. A late Saxon timber building has recently been excavated within the walled enclosure, prompting the suggestion that this may have been an early Saxon *burgh*.

4. Carisbrooke: villa   SZ 485880

The villa lies in private grounds and at the time of writing is not open to the public. The site has now been acquired by the Isle of Wight County Council, and it is planned to open it, with an explanatory display, in the mid 1990s.

The villa was excavated in 1859 and left uncovered; it was re-examined in 1970-3, when its deteriorating condition was noted. The large rectangular house had three parallel ranges of rooms, many of them tessellated (in one case over an earlier mortar floor). At some stage the northern end was extended with two new rooms. The main reception room had a fine geometric mosaic with a bowl of flowers as its centrepiece; this, too, was left uncovered and the ensuing frost damage has been badly repaired. Restoration, however, may be possible. At the southwest corner is a well-preserved bath suite.

5. Newport: villa   SZ 501885

The villa is in Newport in Cypress Road, off the A3056. It is in the care of the Isle of Wight County Council.

The villa was excavated in 1926-7 and has been roofed over. Only the main residential building was completely excavated, but other remains found nearby suggest that it was an extensive site. Today the entrance is on the north side of the building, which originally was entered from the south. The house has fourteen rooms and was built on the site of an earlier structure, probably during the second century AD. It was a wood and plaster building and stood on flint and limestone walls, which survive in places. The roof was of heavy stone tiles, some of which can be seen in Room 10. In Room 5 there is a fireplace which has been laid on top of the earlier tessellation. The west wing is the bath suite, three rooms of which have hypocausts in place. The mosaics, where they exist, are mainly geometric.

The presentation of the villa was completely reorganised in 1992 and the display enlarged to accommodate other material, especially Roman, from the island. This was formerly shown in Carisbrooke Castle but latterly has been in store. The grounds include a fine stone-built Roman corn drier recovered from a ploughed field at Newchurch. An attractive feature is a reconstructed Roman garden.

KENT

1. Canterbury *Durovernum Cantiacorum*: town   TR 570150

Canterbury, possibly the cradle of Christianity in the south of England, was named in the Antonine Itinerary of the third century AD. It was also one of the ten *civitas* capitals mentioned in the Ravenna Cosmography in the sixth or seventh century. It stands on the site of a pre-Roman settlement, where the Watling Street crosses the river Stour. Excavations since the Second World War on bombed sites have revealed that it was a tightly packed town with a *basilica, forum*, theatre and two suites of baths.

The defences, consisting of a flint and ragstone wall with a contemporary bank, were built *c.*270-90, later than in other comparable towns. The principal gate was on what is now the line of the Dover road. A small portion of Roman ragstone work can be seen in the jambs of the Quenin postern gate (a) at the far end of the Broad Street car park and also nearby the beginnings in brick of an arch (opposite Lady Wootton's Green). The medieval walls are on the line of the Roman defences, with the modern ring road following the entire circuit. In 1977 it was discovered that the north wall of St Radigund's church (b), in the northern sector, is formed of the core of the Roman wall to its full height of 8.8 metres; the stonework of the battlements is just visible, incorporated into the medieval masonry. In the southern sector, 230 metres north-east of the East station and on the north side of the ring road, the walls pass the Dane John (c), now thought to be a much altered Roman barrow; there was a cemetery beside it, both being originally outside the town and incorporated into it when the Roman walls were built in the third century.

For the visitor, the best feature of Roman Canterbury is in Butchery Lane, in the area of the shopping precinct. This is a portion of a large house (d) which extended west under Butchery Lane and south as far as The Parade. It is 2.4 metres below the present ground level. On show are the walls of the house built about 100 with later added mosaics of possibly third-century date. There is a small site museum, to which it is hoped eventually to transfer the excellent Roman collections from the Royal Museum in the High Street. The theatre (e) stood in the centre of the Roman town, roughly at the junction of Watling Street and St Margaret's Street. A glimpse of the massive stone wall can be had in both Alberry's Wine Bar and the 'Cellar Romana' of Slatter's Restaurant, both in St Margaret's Street.

2. Canterbury: St Martin's church   TR 158577

The church stands 400 metres east of the walls on a turning off Longport, just past the prison on the A257 Sandwich road, and is

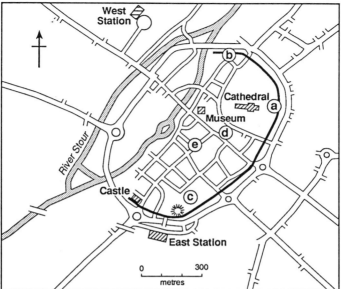

39. *Plan of Canterbury showing the sites described in the text: a, Quenin postern gate; b, St Radigund's church; c, Dane John; d, Roman house in Butchery Lane; e, theatre.*

signposted. A guidebook is available at the church.

This is claimed to be the earliest used church in England — that of Queen Bertha, built before St Augustine's arrival. It could be Roman in origin. The south wall of the nave has courses of Roman brick, and they are used in the right-hand wall of the chancel. The nature of this possibly Roman building is disputed, and — as at Stone-by-Faversham (Kent, 12) — it might have been initially pagan.

3. Dover *Dubris*: forts and Painted House   TR 317426
The Painted House is in New Street, opposite the end of Queen's Gardens, south-west of St Mary's church, and signposted. A guidebook is available.

These remains are sited on what was one side of the Roman harbour, when the coastline was closer to the centre of Dover. A third-century fort of the Saxon Shore series had long been suspected, but its position was unknown until rescue excavations ahead of the York Street relief road in 1970 found the south and west walls. When work commenced on the road it revealed the remains of an unsuspected, earlier, second-century fort on a slightly different site. The remains of over a thousand tiles bearing the stamp *CLBR* show that it was almost certainly the British headquarters of the *Classis Britannica*. The Gallic headquarters of the fleet was at Boulogne. This fort covered an area of over 0.8 hectares, and fourteen major buildings have been postulated as standing within its walls. There was also an extensive *vicus*, or extramural settlement.

The remains of both forts have been reburied under the road, the level of which was raised to preserve them for posterity. However, 3.7 metres below ground level, in a building specially erected to conserve them, visitors can see the remains of one house in the *vicus*. These comprise one complete room, partial remains of a corridor and four other rooms of the 'Painted House', with part of the third-century fort wall and its later bastion.

40. Plan of Dover showing the sites described in the text; 3, the Painted House; 4a, lighthouse; 4b, base of second lighthouse.

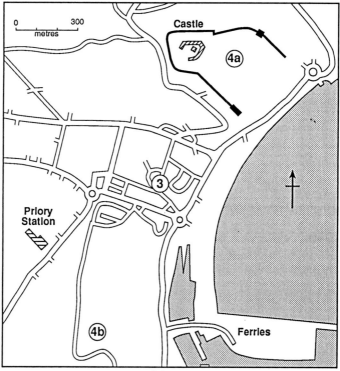

Room 2, which measures 5.5 by 4.9 metres, has all four walls standing to a height of 1.2 to 1.8 metres and all are painted. The lower dado is yellow and green, and immediately above this is a wide band of mottled yellow and pink. Above this the central panels, surrounded by columns painted to look three-dimensional, have designs on a white background. The motifs of these panels start from below the level of the base of the columns. They consist of fronds, torches, trees, wands, human figures and bowls. This is by far the largest area of Roman painted plaster visible *in situ* in Britain. Floors are of *opus signinum*, and a medieval pit in the centre of the floor affords a view of the underfloor heating system. On the exterior of the south side of this room three stokeholes can be seen. The Painted House overlies an earlier building of about 150.

Rooms 3, 4 and 5 were partially destroyed when the Saxon Shore fort was built about 270. Remains of its massive ragstone wall can be seen, as can also the bastion which was added about 300. The painted walls have survived because the masons of the Roman army demolished the house walls at a higher level but left the lowest 1.8 metres intact. These were then buried beneath a bank of earth which backed up the fort wall on the inside. Substantial remains of a bath-house have also been found. It is hoped to preserve this and put it on view.

Further remains of both forts (a gateway of one, a bastion of the other) are now displayed in the nearby historium, 'The White Cliffs Experience', in York Street.

4. Dover: lighthouse   TR 326418

The tower is on the eastern heights inside Dover Castle and at the west end of the church of St Mary in Castro. The castle is open at standard hours, and a guidebook is available.

Dover was probably not the original port of entry to Britain, but as Richborough silted up Dover gained in importance. The lighthouse, or *pharos* (4a), was built as one of a pair on each side of the harbour during the first century AD to guide shipping. In plan it is octagonal with a square interior, faced with greensand and tufa at the base, with a rubble interior and the usual tile courses. Originally it rose as a series of eight stepped stages, like an extended telescope, with a beacon at the top; today it stands to a height of 21 metres but only the lower 13 metres are Roman, the rest being medieval.

The base of the second lighthouse (4b) is on the west hill at Devil's Drop (TR 314401). It was destroyed in the nineteenth century but the site is marked by pieces of masonry taken from it. Reused material shows that this is later than the other lighthouse. Both towers were probably used in conjunction with the Tour d'Odre in Boulogne.

5. Iden Green: ford   TQ 802323

The ford is at the east side of Stream Farm, 800 metres south of the B2086. The most interesting approach is to follow the Roman road from the B2086 down a green track east of Corner Cottages, nearly opposite the entrance to Benenden School. After the first 180 metres the footpath follows along the field edge of the road on its east side. As it descends the hill the road becomes sunken and it approaches Stream Farm. The ford is reached across the modern farm road east of the farm buildings and through a gate straight ahead.

This unusual feature was discovered by the late Dr O. G. S. Crawford and consists of the remains of a paved Roman ford composed of large flat slabs of stone. The paved area was 8.2 to 9.1 metres wide when excavated; in recent years it has been badly wrecked by vandals. A modern boundary stone on the west side helps to locate the ford. Since the road was constructed in Roman times the river has cut through the soil and is now running several feet lower. By crossing over to the south bank the sandstone blocks can be seen tumbled in the bed of the river and projecting from the bank. The course of the road is from Rochester to Hastings via Maidstone, a cross-country route of 60 km.

6. Lullingstone: villa   TQ 529651

The villa lies west of Eynsford village on the left bank of the river Darenth, on a side road off the Dartford to Sevenoaks road (A225). Approach the site either over a picturesque river bridge opposite Eynsford church or under the railway bridge at the station. Most of the main house has been roofed over and it has its own museum and car park. A guidebook is available.

Evidence for a Roman building here was known in 1788, and fieldwork rediscovered the site before 1939; excavation, however, was not possible until 1949 and lasted for twelve years.

The earliest material was Belgic pottery, suggesting occupation of the site before the Roman conquest. The first house, with flint and mortar walls, was built about AD 60; this had a number of central rooms with a verandah and a rear corridor. Roughly a century later a presumably new owner added baths at the west end and a set of basement cult rooms at the other, with a wall painting of three water-nymphs and a water-filled pit in the centre of the floor. The fine marble busts date from this period. The villa was deserted about 200 and reoccupied — after standing empty for half a century — by a farming family, who sealed off the cult rooms, remodelled the baths and built a large barn for the estate. In the fourth century a mausoleum was built behind the house near the site of a circular shrine of the first century, and fine mosaics were laid in the large reception room with its apsidal dining area. They depict the abduction of Europa by Jupiter disguised as a white bull. Bellerophon, mounted on Pegasus, is shown killing the Chimaera with a spear. Around this are dolphins, and female heads representing the four seasons adorn the corners of the mosaic. The portion between these two designs has jumbled geometric patterns, including swastikas.

By about 360-70 the family, or new owners, were Christian and converted the east end of the house to a chapel. The wall paintings include a chi-rho monogram and a frieze of praying figures. This could be regarded as one of the earliest Christian chapels in western Europe. The reconstructed plaster may be seen in the British Museum, with originals of the marble busts: drawings and replicas are displayed on the site.

7. Lympne *Lemanis*: fort   TR 117342
The ruins, known as Stutfall Castle, are in a field south of the main part of Lympne, near the Military Canal. Take the turning marked 'To Church and Castle' and walk down the public footpath to the Military Canal.

The silting up of the coast in this area, forming Romney Marsh, has left this Roman fort site 2.4 km from the present coast. It was one of the forts of the Saxon Shore of late third-century date, though pottery and tiles stamped *CLBR* found in the 1977 excavations confirm that there was a base, still to be found, in the second century. An altar erected by a commander of the British Fleet dates from this earlier phase.

The walls, originally polygonal in plan rather than rectangular, enclose about 4.5 hectares and have been most strangely tumbled by soil movements on the sloping site. They are 3.7 to 4.3 metres thick, with bonding courses and semicircular bastions projecting on the outside. The main gate was in the east wall, and part of this has been left exposed from the 1977 excavations; there was a postern in the west wall.

8. Reculver *Regulbium*: fort   TR 227693
The ruins of the fort and Saxon church are 5 km east of Herne Bay, on the coast north of the A299 at the end of a minor road. The fort walls are always open; standard hours for the church. A booklet is available.

This was originally a small first-century fort defending the northern end of the now silted-up Wantsum channel. It was enlarged as one of the forts of the Saxon Shore, possibly about 220 on the evidence of a dedicatory stone and pottery found in 1960. This later fort covered about 3.2 hectares and has been partly eroded by the sea; this erosion is of comparatively recent date as the fort was complete in the eighteenth century. The walls are 2.4 metres thick but lack the usual bastions and bonding courses — a sign that this fort is relatively early in the series. It is built in the standard pattern with rounded corners. Within, the streets were laid out to grid plan, and outside the walls were two steep ditches. Houses, barracks and headquarters buildings have been located. In 1963 an unusual drying oven was found outside the walls.

The most conspicuous feature of the site is the pair of towers of the thirteenth-century church. Within this there were, until 1809, the remains of the Saxon church; it was then demolished by the vicar. Its foundations have since been outlined on the ground.

9. Richborough *Rutupiae*: fort   TR 325602

The site is 2.4 km north of Sandwich on a side road off the A257. A booklet is available.

This is almost certainly the point of entry of the Claudian invasion in AD 43. At that time it was a natural harbour at the south end of the Wantsum channel, which is now completely silted up. A line of two ditches was dug across the area. Once a bridgehead had been established, these were filled in and timber granaries and stores were built. In about AD 85 these were demolished and a huge triumphal arch clad in white marble was erected, intended as an entry to Britain at the beginning of Watling Street. The base of this can be seen, roughly in the centre of the later fort. Remains of second to third century houses can also be seen. The surrounding triple ditch is of the mid third century, dug at about the time that Saxon raiders first became active. Later the massive walls were erected for the Saxon Shore fort. This final fort covers an area of 2 hectares. The walls have the usual stone and tile courses, rectangular interval bastions (with a postern gate in the north wall) and circular corner towers. Outside is a double ditch to confine attackers to an area which could be covered by fire from the fort.

The amphitheatre is now a hollow, 800 metres south of the fort at TR 321598. It measures 61 metres by 51 metres.

10. Rochester *Durobrivae*: town   TQ 742686

The Roman walls are on the east bank of the river Medway and can be viewed from the Esplanade.

Stretches of the Roman town wall are incorporated in the walls of the castle overlooking the river. The usual courses of carefully cut stone can be seen, with the Norman walls above. The lower parts are modern, replacing stone removed to build Upnor Castle in Elizabethan times. Medieval and modern work meet again at the south-west corner of the Roman circuit in Eagle Court (a public garden), where the Roman wall still stands 3 metres high.

41. Richborough fort, Kent.

It is an addition, probably of the early third century, to a late second-century bank and ditch. The Celtic name suggests that Rochester was built on the site of a pre-Roman *oppidum*; like Canterbury it stands on the Watling Street at a river crossing.

11. Snargate: Rhee wall   TR 015263

The site is on the line of the A259 north-west of Old Romney and the B2080 to Snargate.

The Rhee wall is a piece of Roman civil engineering, originally a large two-walled drainage channel of earth built to carry the bulk of the river Rother from the Appledore area to the sea via Romney. The modern road follows this line. Before its construction the river meandered by Lympne and Hythe, roughly along the line taken by the Napoleonic Military Canal. It was silted up by the end of the fourteenth century and now reaches the sea through the silted Cinque port of Rye.

12. Stone-by-Faversham: mausoleum   TQ 992613

The ruins are about 30 metres north of Watling Street (A2), 2.4 km west of Faversham and opposite the turning signposted to Newnham and Doddington.

The ruins of this medieval chapel incorporate Roman masonry; a square building now forms part of the chancel, where the Roman stones and tile courses can be made out. In the west wall can be seen the stone threshold and the socket for the door. No burial is recorded, but it is believed to have been a Roman mausoleum within sight of the Watling Street and connected with the settlement of *Durolevum* in or near Ospringe. Excavations in 1967 dated it to the fourth century.

LANCASHIRE

1. Lancaster: fort(s) and bath-house   SD 495615
The forts lay beneath and to the south of the Castle. The bath-house is reached from a signposted footpath below the Priory, near the Wery Wall and modern buildings. It is in a railed-off enclosure.

The first fort was of turf and timber, constructed in the late first century and remodelled under Trajan. This was replaced by a stone and timber fort *c.* AD 160. Neither is now visible. This in turn was replaced *c.*330-50 by a massive fortress with at least one bastion. Resembling the rather earlier Saxon Shore series the final fort was a key element in the late Roman coastal defences. The upstanding masonry of the Wery Wall is part of it, as is the short section of V-shaped ditch. The bath-house belongs to the second fort, and was demolished to make way for the final one; the remains are conserved to show the later ditch cutting through the otherwise well-preserved remains of the *caldarium*.

2. Ribchester *Bremetennacum*: fort   SD 649349
The fort is in the modern village.

The fort was originally founded in the early Flavian period. It covered 2.2 hectares and was protected by a clay rampart 6.1 metres wide and a ditch 6.1 metres across. It had timber gateways and angle towers. The fort was rebuilt in stone during the Trajanic period, with a wall 1.8 metres thick. The fort was rebuilt after 197 and continued in use through the fourth century. The visible remains are alongside the site museum and include part of the north wall, the north gate and the front ends of two granaries, probably third-century in date.

The bath-house is behind the White Bull and is signposted from the museum. It was constructed *c.*100 and much modified (including a detached circular *laconicum* or sweating room in *c.*120). It was demolished *c.*200-25.

LEICESTERSHIRE

1. Great Casterton: town   TF 002090
The Roman town is beneath and to the east of the modern village.

This town grew up outside a Roman fort. Sited in a loop of the river Gwash and astride Ermine Street, on which it served as a posting station, it covers 6 hectares and has impressive earthwork defences on the north-east. The town was first defended by a stone wall in the late second century. This was 1.5 metres wide with a coeval 6.4 metres bank behind it and multiple V-shaped ditches in front. After 354, almost certainly on the instructions of Count Theodosius, the wall was equipped with rectangular bastions 5.5 metres wide and projecting 3.5 metres to take catapults, and the multiple ditches were replaced by a single flat-bottomed ditch 18 metres wide. Occupation continued during the Saxon period and early Saxon burials have been found in the tail of the bank.

Immediately to the east of the town lies the Roman fort, revealed by aerial photography and not visible on the ground. 800 metres to the east, a fine mid fourth-century villa was excavated.

2. Leicester *Ratae Coritanorum*: Jewry Wall   SK 585045
The visible remains and the adjoining Jewry Wall Museum are in St Nicholas Street.

Leicester was the *civitas* capital of the Coritani and the walls, no longer visible, enclosed about 40 hectares. The site was occupied before the Roman period, and a fort of the conquest period, probably of legionary size, has been discovered.

The only Roman structure visible *in situ* is the Jewry Wall. It is a remarkable piece of masonry standing 7.3 metres high and forming part of the *palaestra* of the large public baths. They were of sufficient size to accommodate both male and female bathing suites. Hot and warm rooms open off a central hallway which is provided with dressing rooms and lavatories. Adjoining it is the *palaestra*. The baths were begun about 140 and completed about ten years later.

The museum contains the Peacock pavement, originally on view in the cellar of 50 St Nicholas Street, and the Blackfriars mosaic. There is also some fine painted wall plaster.

3. The Raw Dykes: earthwork   SK 584026
The earthwork is on the Aylestone Road, Leicester, between the gasworks and the electricity station.

About 90 metres of this fairly impressive earthwork can be seen, although some 550 metres were recorded in the eighteenth century. Its ditch is 24 metres wide. It has often been suggested that the earthwork formed a leat or aqueduct supplying water to Roman Leicester, but the earthwork lies some 6.1 metres lower than the public baths, 1.6 km distant in the Roman town. It is more probable that the Raw Dykes formed part of a Roman canal, perhaps connected with a dock.

The earthwork was used again in 1645 as a redoubt for Prince Rupert's guns during the Civil War.

LINCOLNSHIRE

1. Ancaster: town   SK 983436
The site is east of Ancaster church and north of the A153.

Ancaster lies in a natural gap in the Lincoln Edge, which in the iron age would have been commanded by Honington Camp hillfort. An iron age settlement has also been located under the modern cemetery in Church Lane.

The Roman walls, probably dating from the early third century, were buried within a rectangular earthwork which measures some 210 by 180 metres and encloses 3.6 hectares. This is only part of a straggling native settlement which lay beside the Ermine Street for 1.6 km between the railway bridge to the north and south of the crossroads at the southern end of the modern village. Within the walled town excavations have found houses with tessellated pavements and underground vaults, but none of these is visible today. The rampart surrounding the south-east part of the town can best be seen in Castle Close beside the A153 road to Sleaford. The only surviving traces of the outer ditch of the town are to be seen in a coppice adjoining the north-east corner of Castle Close.

Beneath the modern cemetery are a mid first-century fort and a late Roman inhumation cemetery. Two Roman stone coffins can be seen at each end of a cemetery path; the stone is local Ancaster limestone, and fairly certainly there was a local stone industry here. Coffins have been excavated which were clearly unfinished, or 'seconds'. A number of finds from the site are in the museums at Grantham, Lincoln and Nottingham University.

2. Caistor: town   TA 117012
A footpath round the east and south sides of St Peter and St Paul's churchyard runs along most of what is left of the Roman town wall.

Little masonry is visible although a massive solid-cored semi-circular bastion juts out below the churchyard wall at a point where the path begins to curve north-westwards; there is a second to the west of this point and substantial remains of another on the north side. Another short stretch of wall lies beside the Grammar School grounds.

The site is very irregular, largely because of its configuration and the presence of springs. Finds from the town are of third- and fourth-century date. A date of about 350 for the defences of Caistor and the larger but similar site at Horncastle (Lincolnshire, 4) seems appropriate. Settlement may have begun in the third century AD.

3. Car Dyke: canal   OS 1:50,000 sheets 113 and 123
The Cambridgeshire sector of this massive work has already

been described (Cambridgeshire, 1). The Lincolnshire part of its course originally ran for 90 km from Peterborough to enter the river Witham at Lincoln. Drainage of the Fens in modern times has often diverted or destroyed its course, but its route can be clearly followed from the Ordnance Survey maps. Although seldom very impressive, it can be seen on the ground at many points; for example, 1.6 km north of the Dogsthorpe level crossing at Peterborough (TF 200033), 1.2 km east of Rippingale station (TF 126283), beside the B1190 at Branston Booths (TF 063690) and at Howell and Ewerby.

4. Horncastle: town   TF 258695
The Roman site is in the centre of the modern town of Horncastle, above the confluence of the rivers Bain and Waring.

This town was probably established early in the conquest, though its stone walls may not have been added until the third or fourth century. It seems to have been rhomboidal in shape, with long sides of 251 metres and short sides of 152 metres and 122 metres. Excavations on the site of a branch library in Wharf Road have revealed a fine section of the wall, which is visible within the library; another section is marked by the south-west angle of St Mary's churchyard, and a third can be seen in Dog Kennel Yard off Lawrence Street. The last has the remains of the circular solid rubble and concrete core of a projecting bastion. Excavation has proved that the walls and bastions are of one build. A section of wall on the south-west side near the school stands barely 3 metres high. Iron age pottery has recently been found within the town.

5. Lincoln *Lindum*: colonia   SK 976719
The limestone ridge forming the Lincoln Edge carried one of the longest prehistoric routeways in Britain. It stretched from Somerset to Yorkshire. In Lincolnshire it was broken by a river gap, later widened as a glacial channel, through which flowed the river Witham eastwards to the Wash. Here was founded a fortress for the IX Legion Hispana about AD 60. This legionary fortress occupied 17 hectares and was defended by at least one ditch and a timber-faced rampart. About AD 90 the same rectangular area was reused as a walled town for retired soldiers and named *Lindum Colonia*. Situated on a plateau, it was surrounded on all four sides by a rock-cut ditch about 24 metres wide. The best preserved section of this ditch (a) is on private land in the garden of Fosse House in Church Lane. Behind the ditch stood the wall, and in East Bight (b) a portion has been exposed by excavation, with an internal tower and an upstanding piece of wall core from which all facing stones have been removed, leaving a core of lime

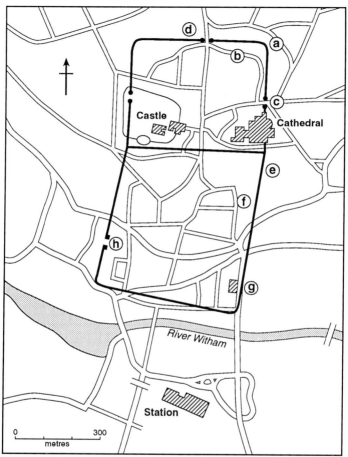

42. Plan of Lincoln showing the sites described in the text: a, Fosse House; b, East Bight; c, Eastgate Hotel; d, Newport Gate; e, Temple Gardens; f, Usher Art Gallery; g, City Museum; h, west gate.

mortar and small limestone blocks some 3-3.7 metres thick. Short sections of wall can be seen in the Eastgate Hotel gardens (c). The core of the wall is also preserved in the garden of Hilton House at the north-east corner of Drury Lane and Union Road. The south wall has been proved by excavation to be immediately south of the Cathedral Close wall in the Diocesan House grounds.

There were gates in the centre of each of the four walls, of which the northern Newport Gate (d) is the most famous. It now consists of a large central arch which spanned a 4.9 metres carriageway, a smaller eastern arch over a 2.1 metres footway, and part of a small western arch of the same size. This is all the inner part of the gateway, the outer northern face having been destroyed by the medieval city gateway. It should be noted that the modern road is about 2.4 metres higher than in Roman times making the arch look lower than it really was. It also had an upper storey.

The foundations of the east gate were excavated in 1959-60 and the northern semicircular gate tower (c) has been consolidated and left on permanent display in front of the Eastgate Hotel in Eastgate. This may have been the main Roman entry into *Lindum*. The gate had two carriageway arches, each 4.6 metres wide.

The west gate was excavated in 1970 and 1971 and found to stand 4.3 metres high. It is to be preserved and opened to the public. All that remains of the south gate is a small section of walling from the carriageway on the west side of Steep Hill.

Towards the end of the second century the *colonia* was extended southwards to take in another 23 hectares. Of the new wall little remains to be seen. At the north-east corner of Temple

43. Lincoln: the Newport Arch.

Gardens (e) it separates the lower garden of the Old Palace from the terraced garden of the Vicar's Court. It is core again, 3 metres thick and more than 4.3 metres high. The ditch in front of it still survives 24 metres wide in Temple Gardens, and another section of the same work (f) can be seen in the gardens of the Usher Art Gallery, Lindum Road. The west gate (h) of this 'lower town' is still preserved in the medieval one, with the remains of two guard chambers flanking the simple carriageway.

Of numerous remains of buildings found within the city, none can be seen today, although the position of a colonnade fronting a Roman street is marked in Bailgate by a row of metal studs. This may represent the forum. The *basilica* is probably represented by a Roman wall, still standing 5.5 metres high, known as the Mint Wall. This is in West Bight, off Westgate, near the Castle Hotel. Many of the objects recovered are displayed in the City Museum (g).

6. Revesby Barrows   TF 303616
These two large round barrows stand beside the A155, 400 metres east of Revesby village.

Both barrows are about 2.4 metres high and 20 metres in diameter. They are surrounded by well-marked ditches. One is reported to have contained a pit cut into the clay containing burnt bones. They could be of bronze age or Roman date, more probably the latter.

44. Lincoln: the Roman west gate of the 'lower town'.

GREATER LONDON

1. London *Londinium*

Roman London was only slightly smaller than the (inner) City of London today and is defined by the line of the Roman and medieval walls. A first visit should start with the Museum of London in Aldersgate Street (nearest Underground station: St Paul's), where leaflets and guidebooks are obtainable.

Londinium was the physical focus of Roman Britain, as a glance at the radiating road system shows, being the upper tidal limit of the river Thames and the lowest suitable bridging point. Colchester, not London (where no pre-Roman settlement existed), was intended by Claudius as the political focus; but London soon became the capital of the province and the Governor's official residence, being first probably a *municipium* and later a *colonia*, renamed *Augusta*. From 197 it was the capital of the new province *Britannia Superior*, and from about 254 onwards the capital both of *Britannia Prima* and the Diocese of the Britains.

The first bridge was some 550 metres upstream of the present London Bridge and was accompanied by an early fort. London's mercantile prosperity developed early and rapidly, initially in the Walbrook area, to fall an easy prey to Boudica's hordes in the insurrection of AD 60-1; substantial deposits of ash are regularly found below the more substantial rebuilding that followed immediately.

The booming prosperity of London received a further check under Hadrian, between 125 and 130, when a further fire swept the city. At least 26 hectares were devastated, reflecting the rapid expansion of the original nucleus. Development, however, continued unabated and by the middle of the second century we can identify the apparatus of a thriving provincial capital: a palace for the *procurator*, a *forum* with the largest *basilica* in Britain (where the provincial council will have met), a temple of the state cult (doubtless dedicated by the council), an extensive street plan, public baths, and possibly an early circuit of defensive earthworks. Unfortunately, none of these features can be seen today. Outside the city at this stage, a sign of status was a masonry fort in the Cripplegate area, later incorporated as a salient in the Roman walls. This presumably served both for transit and onward movement of supplies, and to provide a ceremonial garrison for the Governor. For a century or so this extramural fort was accompanied by an amphitheatre close to its south-eastern corner.

The steady rise of the river seems to have been a problem; recent excavations along the northern waterfront have shown a series of massive timber revetments gradually straightening the

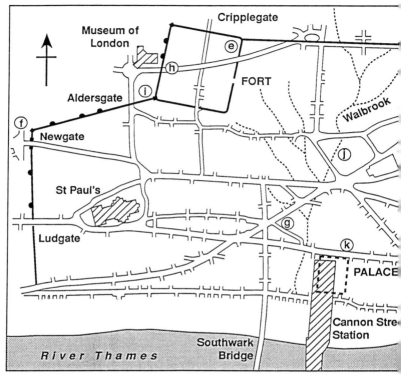

north bank of the river and supporting quaysides, wharves and warehouses. By about 270 the earlier piles were crowned by a substantial wall completing the city defences that had been constructed in the second century. These walls encompassed about 134 hectares, incidentally enclosing a cemetery that had formerly lain outside the city boundaries, as was required by law. London was thus the largest walled town in Britain, at a time when other communities were content with earthen defences. The remains of a boat, found near Blackfriars Bridge, belong to this period; its sea-worn timbers and cargo of Kentish ragstone showed that it had plied to and fro in the Thames estuary bringing stone from the quarries to the new walls. The bastions (or at least some of them) are fourth-century additions designed to carry the heavy artillery that is characteristic of late urban defences.

Two great London museums serve contrasting purposes. The

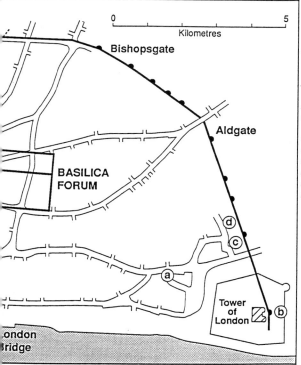

45. Plan of the City showing the sites described in the text: a, All Hallows church; b, Tower of London; c, Wakefield Gardens; d, Coopers Row; e, St Alphage churchyard; f, General Post Office; g, Temple of Mithras; h, Old Street; i, Noble Street; j, Bank of England; k, London Stone.

Museum of London has a remarkable collection of material from the Roman city, including the Blackfriars boat and a model of the waterfront construction. All aspects of everyday life are imaginatively displayed; indeed, from one gallery one looks out on the first view of the Roman walls. The British Museum also has important earlier discoveries from London; but the galleries should be used as an introduction to the wider picture of Roman Britain. Here, moreover, one can set the single province of Britain in the total context of the Roman world.

a. All Hallows church: Roman house   TQ 335807

The church stands between Great Tower Street and Byward Street, a little to the west of Tower Hill. For access to the crypt apply to the verger. A guidebook can be bought at the bookstall.

In the crypt are the remains of the walls of a Roman house with two tessellated floors (originally separated by a wooden partition). There is a very fine model of Roman London in about 400 and a display of Roman pottery, coins and fragments of a figurine of Venus.

b. Tower of London: Roman city wall and waterfront

This fragment of the wall, with a semicircular bastion, stands immediately to the east of the White Tower.

The wall is about 3 metres long, standing to a height of 1.2 metres, and is of Kentish ragstone with tile courses. The bastion which was added to the wall later in the Roman period was rebuilt in the thirteenth century.

Close by, south of the modern History Gallery and next to the Lanthorn Tower, excavations in 1976-7 revealed remains of the massive riverside wall. This has been left exposed to view. It was built about 390 as part of the south-east defence of the city, standing possibly to a height of 6.1 metres. It contains much reused stone and was laced with timbers, the cavity slots for which can be seen.

c. Tower Hill, Wakefield Gardens: wall

The Roman wall here is north of the Tower and is approached via Trinity Square, next to Tower Hill Underground station.

This section stands on the east side of the garden. It is about 15 metres long and in places 6.1 metres high. It is built of ragstone from Kent, with four courses of bonding tile. Above is much rebuilding of medieval date. At the southern end of this section, and less well-preserved, are the remains of half of the foundation of an internal turret. Fragments of the tomb of the *procurator* Classicianus were found in the foundations of the nearby outer bastion in 1852 and 1935, with other inscriptions. The reconstructed tombstone is in the British Museum, and casts of these inscriptions are on view in the Museum of London.

d. Coopers Row: wall

This is to be found in a courtyard behind Midland House, 8-10 Coopers Row, and about 45 metres north of Tower Hill Underground station.

As one enters the courtyard, immediately ahead is the view of the medieval part of the wall with a parapet of about 1200. It has a window and four loopholes for archers. The Roman wall is below, starting at the level of the car park. By leaning over the railings, the whole of this section can be seen, a height of about 4 metres of the wall in squared blocks of ragstone. On the south wall of the courtyard there is a drawing giving more details of this section. Look also through the arch (at the north-east corner) at the outside of the wall, which is complete to its sandstone plinth.

e. St Alphage churchyard: wall and Cripplegate fort

The wall is north of the modern road called London Wall and east of Wood Street. The best view is from the high walk above, viewing from the north-east.

There are no tile courses in the area of the Cripplegate fort, but it will be noticed that there are two parallel walls with a distinct fissure between. The outer wall is the north wall of the fort, while the inner and thicker wall is the later Roman wall built c.200. The outer wall has later work above, of thirteenth- and fifteenth-century date.

f. General Post Office: wall

A portion lies in the GPO yard east of Giltspur Street, but a better portion is in the cellar of the GPO at St Martin's-le-Grand. It may be visited Monday to Friday by permission of the Postmaster.

Most of this curved portion of the city wall is of medieval date. However, next to it on the eastern end is a fragment definitely of Roman date. It is constructed of squared blocks of ragstone with a bonding course of tile and is nearly 2.4 metres thick.

g. Temple of Mithras

The nearest Underground station is Bank (Central and Northern lines).

This 'modern' ruin lies just outside Temple Court in Queen Victoria Street. It is a reconstruction of the Temple of Mithras discovered in 1954 some 55 metres east of its present position, on the site of the present Bucklersbury House. Despite various faults, this reconstruction gives the visitor a good idea of the layout of the Mithraeum. The original building, which consisted of a nave with aisles on either side and a western apsidal sanctuary, was erected sometime in the late second century. Its destruction in the fourth century is sometimes ascribed to Christian fervour.

Finds from the 1954 excavations include a marble head of Serapis, one of Mercury, the head of Mithras and a silver strainer with an elaborately decorated containing box. These are now on display in the Museum of London. The cult of Mithras was introduced to Rome in 68 BC and spread to Britain both through

111

the army and (as doubtless in this case) among the eastern merchants. A marble relief of Mithras killing the bull, which at the same time is being bitten by a snake, a dog and a scorpion, was found nearby in the Walbrook in 1889.

h. Old Street: Cripplegate fort, west gate
This may be viewed on application to the Museum of London.

Here is preserved in part the remains of a double gateway and in its north turret is a guardroom.

i. Noble Street: Cripplegate fort
On the west side of Noble Street at cellar level can be seen the walls of the fort with a number of internal turrets.

At the south end is the corner which explained the curious shape of the city wall. This is a larger tower foundation than the rest and set askew from the general line. This is the south-west corner where the fort wall runs east and the city wall leaves the fort in a south-westerly direction.

j. Bank of England: mosaics
One mosaic can be seen only by appointment, in the private museum of the bank; for the other, enquire at the entrance hall.

These two mosaics were found in 1923 and 1934 during rebuilding, and neither is *in situ*. Both are geometric, and a third, found in 1805, is now in the British Museum.

k. London Stone: milestone
The London Stone is now built into the wall of the Bank of China on the north side of Cannon Street next to St Swithin's Lane, a few yards from its original site.

This battered and uninscribed stone has traditionally been known as a Roman milestone and has been resited more than once in modern times; it has even been suggested that it might have marked the focus of the road system in Britain. If so, it would have formed part of a monumental structure.

2. Greenwich Park: building   TQ 392774
The remains lie at the east end of Greenwich Park, midway between Maze Hill and Vanbrugh gates. A small piece of tessellated floor can be seen in a railed-off area.

The site was dug in 1902 and reported as a villa. It has since been interpreted as a temple, a staging post and a pay place for soldiers. The finds were all mixed up and contained three hundred bronze coins ranging from Claudius to Honorius (i.e. AD 41-423), suggesting use over a long period. Inscribed stones were among the finds. A small rescue dig in 1978, after the removal of dead elm stumps, relocated the superimposed floors. It is expected that the trees will not be replaced.

3. Keston: Warbank cemetery   TQ 415632
This site, in the care of the London Borough of Bromley, is situated 6 km south of Bromley, on the right-hand side of the A233 on the bend after the junction with the B265. Take the road to Keston Foreign Bird Farm. It is open at reasonable times on application, preferably beforehand, to the manager of the bird farm: telephone 0689 52351.

This site was first recorded in 1815 as 'a large elevated tumulus'. It was excavated in 1828 and found to contain a massive circular structure with a building on the north side. Subsequent excavations took place in 1893, 1951-3 and 1961. In 1967 the deteriorating site was totally excavated and consolidated.

Two main tombs were relocated and consolidated; both had been emptied by previous excavations. Tomb 1 is circular and about 8.8 metres in diameter, with walls of flint and rubble 0.9

46. Keston, Greater London: the Roman mausoleum.

metres thick. Originally it may have stood to a height of 6.1 to 9.1 metres, and the presence of six external buttresses suggests that it was earth-filled. No sign of an entrance doorway was detected in the remains. The second tomb was rectangular, 4.6 by 3.6 metres, but was buttressed on one side only. It contained a pit which could have held a stone coffin that was removed in the nineteenth century. A quantity of tiles was found on the south side of the tomb, and it could therefore have been roofed. Outside twelve other burials were found, three of which were cremations in urns. Between the buttresses of the first tomb a small cremation tomb was found in a tile-built cist, secured by pink mortar. Within was a rectangular-lidded lead casket which contained the cremation. Both the box and the lid were decorated with bead-and-reel ornament. Pottery suggested that the cemetery was in use between 180 and 300. The site of a Roman villa lies lower down the slope of the hill.

4. Orpington: building   TQ 454659
The site is on the A232 to the west of Orpington station, in a bank close to the council offices.

The site was found in 1926 during the construction of the council offices and was excavated in 1954-7. The Roman building was built about AD 80 on top of an iron age hut of first-century BC date. Occupation continued into the fourth century. Coarse red tessellated floors were laid over the earlier *opus signinum* floors. A small area has been restored and can be seen between flower bushes. Finds from this site are in the London Borough of Bromley Museum, The Priory, Orpington.

5. Orpington, Fordcroft: bath-house   TQ 467676
The building lies between Poverest Road and Bellefield Road and is under a cover. Viewing may be arranged by prior application to the Curator, London Borough of Bromley Museum, The Priory, Orpington: telephone 0689 31551.

The presence of two Roman buildings within 2 km of each other suggests that the Romans found the western slopes of the Cray valley attractive. Excavation of a Saxon cemetery in 1972 revealed that the cemetery had encroached upon and disturbed an area of Romano-British occupation dating from the first century to the fourth. The building that was excavated measures about 13 by 6.4 metres, with walls still standing some 1.2 metres high in places, and dates from the third century. Two complete rooms and part of a third have been consolidated and protected by a cover. They are part of a bath-house, and the remainder is under the adjoining road. Finds from the excavation are in the Bromley Museum.

GREATER MANCHESTER

1. Castleshaw *Rigodunum*: forts   SD 998096

Both forts are north of the A62 immediately north of the reservoirs north-east of Delph.

Situated on the south-west slope of the Pennines, the site consists of two forts, one inside the other. The outer, earlier fort is Agricolan in date and originally measured 110 by 91 metres, covering about 1.5 hectares. Its turf and clay rampart is still 5.5 metres thick in places and is doubled from the north to the south-west corner. At each corner was a raised rough stone tower or platform.

The inner fort is much smaller, measuring 55 by 46 metres. Its defences were of turf and clay, but its interior included at least one stone building. The fort is Trajanic in date and was abandoned about 125.

The name *Rigodunum* means 'royal fort' and may indicate the presence nearby of the lost headquarters of the Brigantian queen Cartimandua.

2. Manchester *Mamucium*: fort   SJ 835975

The fort lies in the heart of Manchester, on the south side of Liverpool Street (off Deansgate), in public gardens opposite the Manchester Air and Space Museum.

47. Manchester: the inside of the reconstructed defences.

Intensive excavation since the 1960s has elucidated a sequence that reflects military movements in north Britain. It began with an Agricolan fort consisting of a turf rampart and timber buildings *c*.79, reoccupied and refurbished for a further campaign in *c*. 90. This was replaced by a similar but larger Antonine work of *c*. 160 following the suppression of the Brigantes in 150. Rebuilding in stone is dated to the early third century. Meanwhile a substantial *vicus* or civil settlement had grown around the fort, constructed first in timber and subsequently in stone.

Part of the defences and the north gate of the third-century fort have been imaginatively reconstructed on the original foundations. The inscriptions are based on those from other sites, and the proportions reflect current thinking better than the comparable exercise at Cardiff (South Glamorgan, 3). Marked out on the site are three buildings of the *vicus*, contemporary with the stone phase of the defences.

NORFOLK

1. Brancaster *Branodunum*: fort   TF 782440

The fort is 800 metres east of Brancaster crossroads. Take the side road on the north of the A149 to Burnham Deepdale.

Little remains of this fort, which is likely to prove disappointing to most visitors. It stands about 12 metres above sea level and may have been close to a tidal inlet in Roman times, although the coast is now more than a mile away. It originally enclosed 2.4 hectares, but its walls, once 2.7 metres thick, were systematically destroyed about 1770 and now no stonework is visible. The deep hollows of the external fort ditches can be seen on the east and west. On excavation these were shown to be 14 metres wide and 2.4 metres deep. The southern wall lies buried just inside the field and not under the A149. There were gates in the east and west sides and an internal tower in the north-west corner. It was a Saxon Shore fort of third-century date and is known to have been occupied by Dalmatian cavalry about 400. Aerial photography has shown extensive civil settlements to the east and west of the fort.

2. Burgh Castle *Gariannonum*: fort   TG 475046

A minor road from Great Yarmouth leaves the junction of the A12 and the A143. The footpath to the fort can be very muddy in wet weather. The site is in the guardianship of English Heritage and is open at standard times. A guidebook is available.

The Roman fort of the Saxon Shore called Burgh Castle stands on the west side of the present village, 9.1 metres above the marshy estuary of the Waveney. The fort is oblong in shape and encloses about 2 hectares. It now has walls on three sides only, the fourth (western) wall having slipped down the slope. The remaining walls are of mortar-bound rubble with an outer face of flints and tiles. They stand 4.6 metres high, are 1.5 metres thick at the top and 3.4 metres thick at the base and were probably constructed some time after 275. Alterations were made almost immediately and six bastions were added, one at each of the two corners, two on the longest north-south side and one on each of the north and south walls (both of the latter have fallen outwards). Large sockets in the summits supported powerful revolving *ballistae* (catapults). The only surviving entrance, 4.7 metres wide, is in the middle of the eastern wall. Excavation has shown that the fort was destroyed in the middle of the fourth century.

In the seventh century Burgh Castle was probably the Roman fort site, at that time called *Cnobheresburg*, given by the East Anglian king Sigeberht to the Irish missionary St Fursa for the foundation of a monastery. After the Norman Conquest the walls were used as the bailey of a castle with a motte (now removed) in the south-west corner.

3. Caister-by-Yarmouth: town   TG 517123

A small Roman town and port were founded here about 125 close to a sheltered harbour on the southern side (now silted up). Such a port was ideally suited for trade with the continent. The town was at first defended by a wooden palisade backed by a clay bank, but this was replaced about 150 by a flint wall. The palisade is marked in concrete with two post-settings for a wooden bridge. Just inside the southern gate a large seamen's hostel, perhaps with its own laundry, was constructed towards the end of the second century and continued in use for about two hundred years. Part of the foundations of this building as well as a section of the town wall and south gateway have been preserved by English Heritage and can be visited at standard times.

4. Caistor-by-Norwich *Venta Icenorum*: town   TQ 230035

The site is 5 km due south of Norwich Castle, on a minor road from Caistor St Edmund to Stoke Holy Cross. Visitors are not permitted to walk over the ploughed interior or on the walls, except near the church.

Forced into Roman subjection after their revolt under Queen Boudicca in AD 60-1, the Iceni were rehoused in *Venta Icenorum*, an administrative centre and market town constructed on the east bank of the river Tas about AD 70. Although a grid pattern of streets was laid down, dividing the town into blocks or *insulae*, for many years only native huts grew up beside them. About 125 a *forum* and *basilica* were built of stone on a site some 60 metres

48. Caister-by-Yarmouth, Norfolk: the seamen's hostel.

wide, with a colonnade in front facing east. At the same time a
suite of public baths was built inside the town, above the river
into which they drained. New Roman-style houses were erected
about this time, and a pottery industry flourished. At some
unknown date, town walls measuring 335 by 430 metres were
constructed, enclosing some 14 hectares and reducing the size of
the town by about a quarter. These walls stood 6.1 metres high
and were 3.4 metres thick, backed by an earthen bank and with a
ditch 24 to 30 metres wide outside. The wall was of concrete,
faced with squared flint and brick. There were U-shaped bastions
at intervals all around it. The base of one can still be seen on the
west side near the river. The wall was broken by gates in the
centres of the four sides, and wooden bridges carried the roadways
over the ditch. Two Romano-Celtic temples were also constructed about this time. By the end of the fourth century the town
had fallen into disrepair and decay, and although a Saxon cemetery was uncovered immediately south of the walls no settlement
of that period has yet been found.

Today only the great ditch and impressive earthen rampart can
be seen surrounding the site. The whole of the interior is farm-
land, save for the south-east corner where the church of St Edmund,

built out of Roman materials, stands. A number of excavations have been conducted on the site, and many of the finds can be seen in the Castle Museum, Norwich.

5. Peddar's Way, Fring: road TF 733343

It is possible to walk a fine section of the Roman road called the Peddar's Way, south from Fring for about 21 km to Castle Acre (TF 817154). The last 5 km can easily be travelled by car from Shepherd's Bush. Nearer Fring there are scattered round barrows of probable bronze age date close to the track.

NORTHAMPTONSHIRE

1. Irchester: town SP 917666

The site is alongside the A45 Cambridge-Northampton road, north of the village.

This was a small township in the Nene valley, 8 hectares in extent, of which little is visible today except traces of a bank and ditch on the north. The site was first occupied during the Claudian period; this open settlement was later defended by a bank 12 metres wide built between 150 and 200. A mortared wall of limestone 2.4 to 3 metres thick was later added, with an internal turret at the south-west corner. The defences were probably remodelled in the fourth century, when a wide ditch was cut and the west gate blocked. Traces of many buildings have been found from time to time, including a square temple in the centre, and a cemetery was discovered outside the town to the north-east during construction of the railway in 1873.

2. Towcester *Lactodorum***: town** SP 694484

The Roman town lay on either side of Watling Street and was bounded on the east by the river Tove.

This small Roman town was fortified in the late second century, although an open settlement had existed for many years previously. A section of the earthen defences can be seen at their north-west corner behind the police station. By the fourth century the defences seem to have fallen into disrepair.

NORTHUMBERLAND

The following sites in Northumberland are described in the section on Hadrian's Wall: Black Carts, Brunton, Carrawburgh, Carvoran, Castle Nick, Cawfields, Chesterholm, Chesters (bridge abutment; fort and bath-house), Corbridge, Greatchesters, Heddon on the Wall, Housesteads, Limestone Corner, Winshiels.

1. Chew Green: camps NT 787085

Turn right into Redesdale army camp off the A68 1.6 km north-west of Rochester. Permission to enter must be sought from the duty officer. Take the right-hand road north from the camp centre, following the line of Dere Street. Just after Featherwood Farm take the left fork, and immediately after a sharp left turn, turn right. This road climbs over a high pass and the Chew Green complex can be seen across the valley.

The Chew Green earthworks are very complicated and perhaps, as their excavator suggested, best left to the connoisseur. Camp 1 occupies the prime position and was constructed in Agricolan times (*c.* AD 80) to house a full legion. In the mid second century a temporary camp (Camp 2) was built north of the earlier earthworks. Camp 3, inside Camp 1, suggests a semi-permanent site by its substantial ramparts, still 0.9 metres high, and metalled roads. The inhabitants of this site erected Camp 4 to the east, a small permanent fortlet with triple ditches on all sides but the south. On this side are two annexes which were used as wagon parks, with entrances to Dere Street. This camp clearly housed a small garrison protecting the route over the remote moorland.

2. High Rochester *Bremenium*: fort NY 834987

Turn right off the A68 by the war memorial in Rochester village. The cottage opposite has two catapult balls and several Roman gutter stones built into its porch. The road continues to the hamlet of High Rochester and the site of the fort.

The fort of *Bremenium* was founded by Agricola, rebuilt in stone by Lollius Urbicus, reconstructed under Severus and again in the early fourth century. The third-century defences were notable for the multiple ditch system, with artillery batteries on the north and west sides. The remains now visible are of the fourth century and include the interval tower between the south gate and the south-west angle of the fort, and the west gate. The massive masonry of the towers can be clearly seen at the latter. At the north-west angle are the foundations of three superimposed fort walls representing the restorations of 139, 205-8 and 247. The south sides and jambs of the north and south gates are visible, as is the ditch system preserved between the north and east gate and Dere Street passing to the east.

685 metres south of the fort, along the line of Dere Street, were the remains of Roman tombs lining the road. To see the sole survivor take the road back to Rochester village until you reach the third field gate on the left. Continue through the fields for about half a mile until you meet the low *agger* of Dere Street: turn right along it, and the circular tomb can be seen on the right before you reach an outcrop of rocks.

3. Risingham *Habitancum*: fort NY 895861

The site is on the left of the A68, south of West Woodburn. Access is by a farm track from the centre of the village, opposite a lane signposted to East. Woodburn and Monkridge. Permission should be sought at the farm.

Three phases have been identified for this permanent fort. The first belongs to the middle of the second century. This was rebuilt in AD 213 (according to inscriptions now in Newcastle museum) with substantial masonry defences and multiple ditches on two sides. The walls are now grassed over, but much stonework is still visible. This fort served as an outpost for Hadrian's Wall, and further modifications were carried out in the fourth century.

4. Swine Hill: camp NY 904826

20 km north of Corbridge on the A68 (Roman Dere Street), beyond a crossroads signposted Bellingham and Knowesgate and on a sharp bend to the right, park by the track and sign 'Private Property, Vickers PLC'. The site is in the field to the left, beyond a small stream.

This small Agricolan temporary camp can be clearly traced, except on the west. Three entrances and the corners of the rampart are identified by concrete markers. The north gate and the north-east corner are especially prominent.

OXFORDSHIRE

1. Alchester: town SP 573202

The site is 3 km south-west of Bicester on the minor (Roman) road branching south of the A421.

This small town is completely ploughed. Only the slightly raised earthwork around it stands above the neighbouring fields to a height of 0.9 to 1.2 metres. The raised causeway of a road can be seen entering the town at the centre of the north side.

2. Kingston Lisle: barrow SU 328882

The barrow can be seen on the east side of a minor road, 800 metres NNE from Kingston Lisle.

The form and position of this barrow suggest that it is of Roman date.

3. North Leigh: villa SP 397154

The villa is signposted off the A4095. It is at East End, not North Leigh. There is a short walk from the car park. The site is in the care of English Heritage and is open daily.

This villa began as a small rectangular building with a detached bath-house. It was later extended and two-colour mosaic floors were introduced. As time went by wings were added, and then in the fourth century the whole house was remodelled as a courtyard villa, with rooms on three sides and an entrance gateway on the fourth. The best-preserved room is the dining room at the western corner of the house. This had underfloor heating and a vaulted ceiling. The walls were painted while the floor bore an elaborate mosaic similar to one at Chedworth. Only low walls remain of the rest of this very large house. Air photographs show that many more buildings remain to be un-covered on the south-west side of the hill.

SHROPSHIRE

1. Wroxeter *Viroconium Cornoviorum*: town   SJ 565087
Take the B4380 or B4394 to Wroxeter, which is south of the A5 from Shrewsbury to Wellington and is signposted.

Viroconium in its prime was the fourth largest city in Roman Britain and its defences enclosed at least 73 hectares.

Only a portion of this vast site, once walled, is visitable today; much remains beneath the surrounding fields. In particular, air photography and excavation in the neighbourhood have revealed marching camps and an early cohort-sized fort. Wroxeter was a base for successive campaigns against the Welsh tribes, notably by the XIV Legion and subsequently the XX. Their legionary fortress lay to the north-west of the exposed remains, partly under the *forum*. The abandonment of the fortress in the 90s led to the foundation of *Viroconium* as the capital of the Cornovii — an event commemorated in AD 130 by the great inscription of which a cast is in the site museum (the original is in Rowley's House Museum, Shrewsbury). The inscription graced the *forum*, now represented by a line of 16 column bases in a grassy hollow. The prosperity of *Viroconium* is shown by the fact that when the *forum* and *basilica* were burned down in *c.*165-85 they were immediately rebuilt on a more grandiose scale.

Viroconium flourished until *c.*250 but then entered a decline similar to that experienced by most Romano-British towns from that period onwards. At the time of the usurpation of Carausius (286) the *forum* and *basilica* were burnt down and never rebuilt. The baths, also damaged in the fire, were repaired and used for a further century. However, life in the city seems to have continued well into the fifth century, for at the beginning of the century the site of the *basilica* was levelled and redeveloped with a new street lined with timber buildings, some of them quite substantial.

The main remains visible at present are on both sides of the minor road which bisects the site; on the east side of this road an area 113 by 67 metres is open for inspection. It includes the conspicuous 'Old Work', one of the largest pieces of upstanding

Roman masonry that survive in the civil zone of Roman Britain. This is part of the public baths of *c*.200, successor to an unfinished bath-house that has been traced beneath the forum to the west. It represents the south wall of a large aisled building that served as the *palaestra* or indoor exercise hall of the baths to the south of it. It collapsed in *c*.350. The complex baths, excavated in the 1860s, are still imperfectly understood, but successive cold, warm and hot rooms with their furnaces can be seen, and — a rare feature — a large open-air swimming pool.

The site is maintained by English Heritage. A handbook is available and there is a good site museum. Note especially some wall plaster from the baths, a stack of samian bowls (the stock of a pottery stall trapped in the ruins of the *forum* colonnade) and a rare fifth-century inscription.

SOMERSET

1. Charterhouse-on-Mendip: settlement ST 500565
The site is south of the B3134 between Burrington Combe and the Castle of Comfort inn, north-west of its junction with the B3371.

Within a few years of the Roman conquest the silver and lead workings, which had been exploited during the iron age, were developed under Roman military supervision. The earliest datable lead pig from the site is dated to AD 49. The general area has yielded eleven lead pigs in all, of which four, inscribed with the name of Vespasian (and now in Wells Museum), were found in 1956 on Rookery Farm (now Vespasian Farm), Green Ore, north of the Roman road from this settlement to Old Sarum and beyond. The chief objective of these mines was, however, probably silver rather than lead.

The visible remains include: three rectangular enclosures (perhaps not all of them Roman), of which at least one was a fort (military equipment has been found in the area); a small amphitheatre at 499565; and an extensive area of mine workings comprising filled-in shafts and hollows. There is so far no known method (short of excavation) of distinguishing between those of Roman and those of medieval and later periods, mining in this area having continued intermittently until the end of the nineteenth century. A street plan (whether Roman, medieval or later) is sometimes visible in the arable fields north-east of the amphitheatre.

2. Cheddar Caves ST 467539 (Gough's Cave)
The most dramatic approach is by the B3135 down the Cheddar Gorge. The chief accessible caves (Gough's and Cox's) are on the left-hand side.

Several of the caves in the Cheddar area have yielded evidence of occupation during the Roman period. A selection of the finds is exhibited in Gough's Cave museum.

3. Ham Hill: hillfort and Roman occupation

ST 480168 (centre)

The hillfort is just south of Stoke-sub-Hamdon on the A3088, west of Montacute.

This is a very large L-shaped hillfort of some 80 hectares. On its north-west spur foundations of a Roman building have been located and the area has yielded military equipment, suggesting a small fort or the headquarters of an imperial estate. During the Roman period (and subsequently) the area was extensively quarried for the celebrated honey-coloured Ham Hill stone, which was used for many Roman buildings in and well beyond this area, and also for Roman coffins. The quarrying was probably done under military supervision, as was usual with mines and quarries.

4. Ilchester *Lindinis*: town ST 520226

Roman and modern Ilchester is at the junction of the A37 and the A303.

This was the northern *civitas* capital of the Durotriges in the later Roman period. As such it was the administrative and market centre for the rich farming (especially cattle-raising) country between Mendip and the Dorset chalk downs. There are numerous Roman villas, some with notable mosaics such as those from Low Ham (in Taunton Museum) and Lenthay Green (in Sherborne New Castle).

A fort was built after AD 90 and levelled sometime after 150. Probably in the late second century the town was enclosed by a clay rampart (still visible in fields to the east), which was later strengthened by a massive stone wall. Ilchester is connected by the Fosse Way with Bath and Exeter and by other Roman roads with Dorchester and over the Polden Hills to settlements north of Bridgwater.

5. Pen Pits: Roman quarries ST 766320 (rough centre)

Approach by the A303 from Mere west through Zeals and then along the byroad to the west.

The site comprises an extensive series of large pits believed to have been for quarrying stones for querns. One of the pits is overlapped by (and therefore is earlier than) the Norman defensive work of Castle Orchard. Excavations in 1833 yielded Roman pottery and quern fragments.

6. South Cadbury: activity in the Roman period ST 628252

Access is from the A303 by road from Chapel Cross to South Cadbury, and then by footpath to the south-west by the post office.

In its final pre-Roman phase this great multivallate hillfort was occupied by the Durotriges, but it was bypassed by Vespasian's advance of *c.* AD 43-4. The Durotrigans continued to live there until *c.*70-80, when there was a Roman assault. The Durotrigans appear to have been forewarned and made preparations by hastily strengthening the defences. The Durotrigans were overcome and some were slain at the entrance. The excavator considers that the Roman assault was more in the nature of a police action than a military one.

A few late Roman coins, considered representative of a larger number that has escaped the archaeological record, and certain other finds are interpreted as implying the former existence within the hillfort of a Romano-Celtic pagan temple of the type which was built in several other hillforts towards the end of the fourth century. No foundations of such a structure have been found, but they may have been removed by stone robbing or cultivation.

7. Wookey Hole Caves   ST 533478
Turn off the A371 west of Wells, to the north end of Wookey Hole village.

The outer part of the Great Cave was occupied intermittently, probably by both adventurers and squatters, especially during the fourth century. Finds, including pottery and bronze brooches, are on show in the Wookey Caves Museum.

STAFFORDSHIRE

1. Wall *Letocetum*: town   SK 100065
Wall is approached via the A5 and is signposted from Brownhills.

The earliest occupation at Wall was a large fort of *c.* AD 50-8, doubtless for part of the XIV Legion. Continuing military occupation will have attracted civilian settlement; this became the small town of *Letocetum*, effectively a posting station beside Watling Street where a hostel and horses were provided for official travellers. Little is known of the town, which covered 8 to 12 hectares. Much of its foundations has been robbed for stone over the past few centuries. Originally it was surrounded by a wall and ditch and must have been a place of some importance.

The main visible remains consist of an elaborate bath-house excavated in 1912-14. A second building was cleared at this time, 12 metres north-east of the baths; this was probably the *mansio*, or hostel. The bath suite consists of several rooms, a furnace and a hypocaust. They are more complete than any other site of a similar nature yet found in Britain. The site is in the care of English Heritage, and a guidebook is available at the site. The small museum contains some interesting Celtic sculptures which should not be missed.

SURREY

1. Farley Heath: temple   TQ 051450
The site is 3 km south of Albury and 8 km south-east of Guildford, on Farley Heath, on the north side of the road.

This was noted as a likely Romano-Celtic temple site by Camden in 1586 and by John Aubrey about a century later. It was dug by Martin Tupper and his team of 'merrie' navvies in 1848, using the site for a treasure hunt. No satisfactory report exists, but the finds were deposited in the British Museum. A spread of iron age coins was found near the temple and there is also a series of British gold coins followed by Roman base issues. Also found were quernstones, slingstones and Roman pottery including samian ware. Two potters' kilns were found, but they are undated. Of great interest are a bronze binding of a ceremonial staff decorated with bronze figurines in repoussé work, and two small candlestands with red and green enamel decoration.

Subsequent excavations in 1926 and 1939 have confirmed the long period of occupation. An inner earthwork about 23 metres square encloses the temple, the outline of which has been preserved. The outer earthwork, which crosses the modern road, is medieval. The temple stands at the possible end of a Roman road which branches in a north-westerly direction from Stane Street at Rowhook.

2. Stane Street: road   TQ 185551
Stane Street crosses the B2033 at this point, 6 km north-west of Dorking.

Stane Street is the name given, since at least 1270, to the Roman road from London to Cirencester. Sectioning the road by excavation at various points along its route has produced pottery which suggests that it was in use by AD 70.

At this point it can be seen running in two directions: north-east through Tyrrells Wood and later Pebble Lane, and on the opposite side of the road as it runs on to the Mickleham Downs. Near Cherkley Court the *agger* of the road can be clearly seen. The road continues down to Burford Bridge. South of Dorking (at TQ 153417) the A29 uses it for a 4 km stretch before the route leaves the county. For a further stretch see West Sussex, 4.

3. Titsey Park: villa   TQ 405546
Take the B269 from Limpsfield to Warlingham. After 1.6 km a drive enters Titsey Park. The site is to the left of the drive, south-west of the lakes. Permission should be sought at South Lodge.

This villa was discovered in 1847 and excavated in 1864. It measures 37 by 18 metres. It consists of two parallel long corridors with an area between which had traces of a red tessellated floor. There are smaller rooms at each end, of which one at the south-west end was painted in red stucco. Coins suggest occupation from 166 to 180 and, after a definite break, again from 320. It is suggested that in this later phase the rooms at the west end were converted for the washing and bleaching of cloth.

The site is now disappointingly neglected and overgrown. Two rooms can still be made out, one with a hypocaust.

SUSSEX: EAST

1. Holtye: road   TQ 462388

The exposed section is at the bottom of a slope on the south side of the road from East Grinstead to Tunbridge Wells (A264, formerly B2110), 7 km east of East Grinstead. Look for the signboard at the entrance to the path, 275 metres east of the public house on Holtye Common. The site is in the care of the Sussex Archaeological Trust, Lewes, and is always open.

This is part of the Roman road connecting London and Lewes, a distance of 71 km. It passes through the ironworking area of the Sussex Weald, which is just to the south. The section at Holtye was excavated in 1939 and from the excavation this stretch, which has been fenced off, has been left exposed for inspection. Iron slag from the Wealden furnaces was used to surface the road. It was found to be over 4.6 metres wide at this point and 305 mm thick in the centre, thinning to 76 mm at the edges. Over the centuries the slag has rusted together to produce a hard surface. When it was first excavated cart ruts were visible in the surface towards the bottom end of this section. A small stream running diagonally across the road left a shallow hollow which can still be made out. There would have been a bridge across the river at the bottom of the slope.

2. The Long Man of Wilmington   TQ 543035

The figure is 5 km north of Eastbourne on the north side of the downs and 1.6 km south of the Lewes-Polegate road, A27. The best general view is from near Wilmington church and priory.

This is a tall long-legged man cut out in the chalk down, approximately 72 metres in length, with arms partly bent, holding a staff in each hand and with feet turned to the left. The figure was last restored and the outline marked in yellow-white brick in 1874. It has been attributed to the Roman period on the basis of its vague resemblance to the figures carrying standards on the

49. Wilmington, East Sussex: the 'Long Man' seen from below.

reverse of Roman fourth-century coins. However, there are also possible connections with Scandinavian legends. In 1964 considerable support for this theory was provided by the discovery of a buckle in a Saxon grave at Finglesham near Deal. This buckle depicts a horned man who holds a spear in each hand and with his feet deflected to the left. The Long Man was probably emasculated under puritan influence in the seventeenth century or later. The only other probably Roman hill figure is at Cerne Abbas (Dorset, 3), and this, too, is human.

3. Pevensey Castle: fort *Anderitum*   TQ 645048
The fort is on the A259 at the west end of Pevensey. It is managed by English Heritage and a guidebook is available.

This 4 hectares fort is one of the Saxon Shore series and was built in the fourth century. It used to be thought, on the basis of two stamped tiles, that it was reconstructed under Honorius (395-423) but tests have shown these tiles to be forgeries. It stands on the clifftop above the marshes approximately 1.6 km from the sea. In Roman times the sea reached the east and south sides of the fort, providing a harbour. The area enclosed is roughly oval, lacking the square corners that were normal for such a fort; it is late in the series and shows how the formality of rigid planning was breaking down. But notice the close spacing of the project-

50. Pevensey Castle, East Sussex.

ing bastions at the east and west ends to give a complete field of fire around the tight corners. One bastion in the north wall stands almost to full height and contains an original artillery embrasure (unfortunately blocked by a machine-gun post during the Second World War).

The walls were 3.7 metres thick and survive in places up to 7.6 metres high. They are missing on the south side, and a section has also fallen on the north side. The main entrance is at the west end and was possibly arched. It is fronted by two strong bastions and has guardrooms on either side behind them. The east gate was of simple type and possibly gave access to the sea. There is a postern gate in the north wall. The walls themselves are built on a foundation of chalk and flint; excavation has shown that they were reinforced with timbers. Above this level, sandstone rubble with string courses of ironstone and green sandstone was used. Building was undertaken by a number of teams of men; the junctions between the sections can be distinguished by the differing sizes and shapes of the stones.

No major Roman buildings have been found inside; the only remains were of wooden huts. Outside the walls at the south-west corner are the remains of a defensive ditch. After the Norman Conquest the keep was built in the south-east corner. The inner bailey was added in the thirteenth century.

51. Pevensey, East Sussex, seen through the Roman east gate.

SUSSEX: WEST

1. Bignor: villa SU 988147

The villa lies east of the village of Bignor on a minor road from Bury to Bignor, 8 km south-west of Pulborough. A guidebook is available and there is a small museum.

The villa was discovered during ploughing in 1811 and excavations followed over a period of eight years. It stands just west of the line of the Roman road from London to Chichester (Stane Street), just before the road climbs Bignor Hill on to the South Downs. The chief buildings, containing hypocausts and tessellated pavements, have been roofed over. The original walls were found to a height of 0.6 metres. They have been built up with rubble from the site. The remainder of the buildings and the surrounding walls, with the exception of the cold bath, have been reburied.

The chronology of the site was not established by early excavation. Recent work in 1956-61 revealed iron age and Roman first-century pottery on the site and an early timber building under the west wing. The house was built at the end of the second century and after a fire was rebuilt in stone. This simple corridor villa was enlarged into a courtyard villa in the early fourth century. With its enclosing wall and outbuildings the villa must by this time have covered nearly 1.8 hectares.

The mosaic pavements, although damaged by tree roots, are very fine. The one depicting Ganymede was the first discovered on the site. Another noteworthy subject is Venus and cupids as gladiators in the Apsidal Room. There are two with geometric designs and a fine floor with a head of Winter wearing a cloak and hood. A 24 metres length of geometric tessellation, flooring the corridor, has recently been added to the mosaics on view. The source of the water supplying the baths and the ornamental basin in the centre of the main reception room has not been discovered.

There is a site museum and a guidebook is available.

2. Chichester *Noviomagus Reginorum*: town SU 865047

The name ('Newtown') suggests that the town had no pre-Roman origins. Recent excavations have shown that there was a military presence at the conquest period. It was, however, the place where Tiberius Claudius Cogidubnus, client king of the Regini (or Regni), established his new capital. Built into a wall of the Council House in North Street is a large inscription found in 1723. It is hard to read and parts are missing, but it was evidently the dedication of a temple to Neptune and Minerva, erected by a guild of shipwrights; it records the name of Cogidubnus and gives his title as 'Great King' — a title implying the favour of the

Senate and the Emperor.

As the *civitas* capital of the Regnenses the town received its street plan about AD 75-85, and when it was enclosed by defences about 200 it was 40 hectares in size. The general shape is polygonal, similar to Silchester (Hampshire, 8). Later, in the fourth century, the walls were given bastions and the whole circuit was much refaced in the medieval and later periods. Outside the walls, in Whyke Lane North, there are remains of an earthen amphitheatre, 70 by 58 metres.

To the north of Chichester there are extensive linear earthworks running for miles. These are the Chichester Dykes and appear to have been for the protection of Bosham harbour and the approach to the Selsey peninsula, where there was a large pre-Roman *oppidum* now lost to coastal erosion.

Material from Roman Chichester is in the museum, in Little London. The only remains visible in the town are a panel of mosaic in the cathedral and a fragment in Morant's shop, West Street.

3. Fishbourne: palace   SU 838047

2.4 km west of Chichester turn north off the A27 into Salthill Road (signposted 'Roman Palace'). The site is in the care of the Sussex Archaeological Trust, and there are a museum and café on site. A guidebook is available.

Tesserae disturbed by a pipe trench in 1960 led to the excavation of this, one of the most remarkable buildings in Roman Britain. The site was first occupied by the military granaries and storehouses of a short-lived supply base of the conquest period (AD 43). Once these had been removed, work started on a timber 'villa' of two separate buildings; their owner moved in about AD 50, while architects and builders set about its immediate replacement in masonry a few yards away. Its successor was, in effect, a small palace with a colonnaded garden, bath suite and *palaestra*, living rooms with mosaics and painted walls, and servants' quarters; this was ready by the early 60s. In the new province such luxury was remarkable enough; but before long the best Italian architects were planning to eclipse this 'protopalace' and incorporate it into what we see today — a palace reflecting the latest Mediterranean tastes in materials, workmanship and design. (A shortage of hypocausts, however, betrays an ignorance of the British climate.) It was a residence fit for a king, as the audience chamber, or throne room, in the state rooms of the west wing seems to suggest. The excavator interpreted this magnificence as Rome's gift to its loyal client king Cogidubnus; a review of the dating evidence has suggested a high-ranking Roman official in the new provincial government as another possibility.

This 4 hectares masterpiece consisted of four wings enclosing a formal garden, with servants' quarters beyond and a private park sweeping down to a small private harbour; there may have been a large estate, but this was no villa in the normal, agricultural sense. Visitors from nearby Chichester would have crossed a small bridge to enter the colonnaded entrance hall in the east wing, flanked by luxurious residential apartments. Before them at a slightly higher level, stood the west wing seen across the garden, dominated by the steps and matching portico of the audience chamber. To the left lay the south wing, the private apartments; to the north an ingenious arrangement of twenty-three rooms around two private, colonnaded gardens that could be allocated to two, or three, distinguished guests and their entourages. Even visiting senators must have marvelled at the mosaics, the inlaid walls and the paintings in this barbarian corner of the empire.

By the end of the first century, however, king Cogidubnus had died and his kingdom was incorporated into the province. It seems that the palace was promptly split up into separate units — for whom, we shall never know. Bath suites, with hypocausts, were inserted into the north and east wings, and polychrome mosaics laid. The result anticipated the great luxury villas of later Roman Britain by about two centuries; by the end of the third century the builders were at work yet again on a major remodelling when a fire, doubtless started accidentally, swept the entire creation into the oblivion from which the unsuspecting bulldozer driver rescued it in our own day.

The visitor today sees one half of the main site. The A27 bisects it, and two lines of modern houses and a public house have obliterated the entire south wing and half of the garden. All the north wing, however, is open to view beneath an elegant modern structure that is itself a masterpiece; the north-west corner (where you enter) contains a compact and informative museum. The mosaics are a notable feature, especially that showing Cupid on a dolphin. An earlier geometric pavement with a rare 'city wall' border was discovered below it in 1980; this is displayed separately nearby. Further mosaics from other sites (e.g. Chichester and the Chilgrove villa) are now displayed here. The garden has been recreated in its original form as far as the evidence of excavation and background research will allow.

4. Stane Street: road   SU 940106
8 km north-east of Chichester Stane Street crosses a side road signposted to Eartham from the A285. On the north side where the road bends there is a forest car park in Eartham Wood. The Roman road can be walked north-eastwards and south-westwards from here.

The *agger* of Stane Street is clearest to the south-west of the modern road, from where it can be followed as a footpath for 1.2 km to the A285. A few hundred metres on, the A285 leaves the Roman line, which continues across the side of Halnaker Hill as a footpath and bridleway to Warehead Farm (916087).

To the north-east the 6 km walk to Bignor Hill starts as a forest ride preserving the *agger* and gravelled surface of Stane Street, becoming a footpath on or beside the line past Gumber Farm. The route is less clear past the summit of Bignor Hill (where the signpost is south of the true line). Beside the metalled road down into Bignor village note the terrace of the Roman road below it, and (at 977133) there is a branch to the Bignor villa (West Sussex, 1) diving steeply down the hillside northwards.

A further stretch can be traced south-west from Pulborough Bridge (TQ 043180) running as a causeway across the Arun marshes with the footpath at its northern side. West of the level crossing the now disused Midhurst branch of the railway was built upon the *agger*, passing through the faint earthworks of Hardham posting station at 031175.

For a further section of this road see Surrey, 2.

52. *The gravelled surface of Stane Street, West Sussex.*

TYNE AND WEAR
Three sites in Tyne and Wear are described in the section on Hadrian's Wall; they are Wallsend, Benwell and Denton.

1. South Shields *Arbeia*: fort   NZ 365678
The fort is reached by the B1302, which circles the northern area of South Shields. The site is signposted. There is a small museum but no car park. A leaflet is available on the site, which is in the care of the Tyne and Wear County Council.

The fort of *Arbeia* was sited to control the port in the mouth of the Tyne, and it owes its unusual character to its use as a supply depot for sea-borne goods. It was originally a Hadrianic fort, and about 162 an extra granary was added. For the Severan campaigns in the north (208-11) a major reconstruction took place, turning the fort into a supply base with four barracks and twenty-two granaries. Also early in the third century four of the granaries were converted into barracks for junior officers and occupation continued to the end of the fourth century.

Excavation and conservation are in progress on a large area of the fort, to which more has been added recently. Parts have been grassed, but much is displayed with the Hadrianic and Severan phases distinguishable. Much of the fort wall and three gates are now visible, with the *principia* and several granaries.

Part of the defences and the west gate have been reconstructed on the original foundations. As at Cardiff (South Glamorgan, 3) the actual height may have been overestimated, and some details (such as the superstructure of the towers) are highly conjectural. Nevertheless, the fine site museum and the extensive view from the top of the tower provide an excellent introduction to Roman military planning — bearing in mind that in its visible form this was not a typical working fort but rather a specialised store-base for the Severan campaigns in Scotland.

WARWICKSHIRE

1. The Lunt, Baginton: fort   SP 346752
The fort is in the village of Baginton, immediately south of Coventry and near Coventry airport, accessible via the south-east end of the Coventry bypass.

This important site is owned by Coventry Corporation and systematic excavation and reconstruction by Coventry Museum began in 1966. The original object was to investigate a 'typical' Roman fort, but the site proved completely untypical. The eastern defences, the first to be examined, were found to curve to accommodate a circular *gyrus*, or training ground for cavalry mounts, 33 metres in diameter. The fort was clearly a cavalry base, constructed shortly after the Boudiccan revolt, presumably as a base for the reprisal campaign. It was subsequently replaced by a 1.8 hectares fort, which was occupied for some twenty years before abandonment. Two centuries later there was a brief reoccupation, evidenced by a rebuilding of the defences with a massive earthen bank, a U-shaped ditch and a substantial gateway.

So far, a stretch of the earlier ramparts, the east gateway and one of the granaries have been reconstructed, as well as the *gyrus*. The granary now forms the site museum.

WILTSHIRE

1. Littlecote: villa   SU 300704

Approach from the B4192 and the byroad between Chilton Foliat and Froxfield, and proceed along the drive past Littlecote House, west of which is the villa, which is now excavated and conserved. It lies just south of the river Kennet. The villa is open to the public from Easter to September in 1993. For information on whether and when it will be open in subsequent years, telephone 0488 684000.

This is one of an extensive group of villas surrounding the small Roman town of *Cunetio* (Mildenhall), east of Marlborough. The fine Orpheus mosaic was discovered in 1730 by William George, then steward on the estate. It was covered over soon afterwards, but careful drawings were done beforehand for a published engraving, and an embroidered tapestry, reproducing the design fairly accurately on a scale of 1 inch to 1 foot, was done by Mrs George and now hangs on the wall of one of the rooms at Littlecote House. The finding of loose *tesserae* in 1976 led to excavation and rediscovery of the mosaic from 1978 onwards. It measures 12.5 by 8.5 metres.

The mosaic is in two parts. One is a geometric four-panelled design bordered on opposite sides by a *crater* with opposing figures of panthers on one side and a cantharus with opposing sea-leopards (?) and dolphins on the other side. The other part, divided from the first by a narrow rectangular panel, comprises a square bordered on three sides by semicircular apses. The square encloses two concentric circles, the innermost containing a figure, variously interpreted as Orpheus or Apollo, playing a lyre of four strings but with room for a fifth; to the right of this lyre is a small canine animal. The area between the inner and outer circles is quartered, each quarter containing a female figure riding an animal, perhaps representing the four seasons. The mosaic was in poor condition when rediscovered, and it has been convincingly restored using the original *tesserae* and replacement ceramic materials. It is undoubtedly one of the finest Roman mosaics in southern England.

The building seems to be an independent wing of the villa, a fourth-century conversion of an aisled barn into a cluster of rooms with an open court. Interpretation of this complex is controversial, and much depends on the identification of the central Orpheus/Apollo figure. One view sees this as an unheated dining room, presumably for summer use, of a three-lobed form familiar in the Mediterranean but unique in Britain. A more ambitious hypothesis identifies this as a cult centre for the Orphic mysteries, in which a ritual meal played a part. The search for symbolic detail in the mosaic then becomes important.

The mosaic is in Building 1 and has until recently been un-covered during the summer months. The remaining buildings 2-7 lie on three sides of a large, partly walled courtyard and should be visited in an anticlockwise direction. Building 2 (c.170, modified c.280 into a workshop and workers' house) adjoins Building 3, the main villa house (a much modified corridor plan including a bath suite). At its south-west corner is a single-roomed cottage (Building 4), and due west of it, incorporated in the courtyard wall, is Building 5, a possible shrine. Building 6 is a large early third-century barn, modified c.270-80 with a central line of pillars and a small bath suite. Note the pillared entrance-porch. The east range incorporated a possible stable, and the gateway (Building 7) was a substantial towered structure with a probable granary over it.

The overall appearance of the complete fourth-century complex must have been very impressive, with at least five towers as high as 12.2 metres dominating the roofscape. Two flanked the main gateway, one at either end of the main house and one above Building 1.

2. Rotherley and Berwick Down: settlements

ST 948196 and 941197

Take the B3081 to Tollard Royal and then the bridleway due north for about a mile. The earthworks of Berwick Down are to the right of the track. From here strike due east across the valley for 800 metres — there is no footpath — to reach Rotherley.

These two are typical of the iron age and Romano-British native settlements of Cranborne Chase and should be visited with nearby Woodcuts (Dorset, 11). At Berwick Down a U-shaped earthwork encloses a hut site, a single-family unit; this first-century AD site contrasts with a larger circular enclosure about 30 metres to the north where the cluster of rectangular house platforms suggests a small community. These are Romano-British, whereas further earthworks to the north are of the iron age.

The earthworks at Rotherley are finer, because after excavation in 1885 by General Pitt-Rivers they were, like nearby Woodcuts, restored by him. Occupation here began in the iron age and continued with little material change until the end of the third century. Today we see a large circular enclosure with a single entrance and funnel-shaped outworks; this enclosure held a single, large hut, while a smaller compound north-east of it was used for the threshing and storing of grain and other jobs. The adjoining earthworks defined fields and separated arable from pasture.

YORKSHIRE: NORTH

1. Aldborough *Isurium Brigantum*: town   SE 406664

Much of the site of the *civitas* capital of the Brigantes lies under the modern village of Aldborough. It began as a fort in the first century AD but by 150 was a flourishing township. Its walls, built in the second half of the second century, surrounded an area of 24 hectares. They were of red sandstone with an earthen rampart behind and a 43 metres ditch on the north side. Parts of the north gate, two huge blocks of millstone grit, are still *in situ*. The wall was 2.7 metres thick, with rectangular interval towers. Part of the city wall, maintained by English Heritage and 275 metres long, can be seen behind the museum.

In the fourth century much of the town was rebuilt and its defences were reorganised. The wall was given large angle bastions and a new ditch cut. Many mosaic pavements found in the town date from this period. Two of them can be seen in the garden behind the Aldborough Arms. Others are in the Leeds City Museum. Of twelve found, five are still *in situ*, some beneath the vicarage and manor house. One of the crudest but most famous, illustrating the legend of Romulus and Remus, is in the Leeds City Museum. The town continued to flourish to the end of the fourth century, and perhaps later. An earthwork called Studforth Hill, outside the English Heritage enclosure, may possibly be the town amphitheatre.

2. Cawthorn: camps   SE 784900

Access is via a minor road leading east from Cropton. Park 180 metres east of the turning to 'Keldo only', where a track leads north to the sites at 778894. They are best visited in winter when the bracken is low.

These military works were built on the edge of the Tabular Hills. Camp 1 is on the west. It is a roughly square earthwork enclosing 1.4 hectares, defended by double ditches. On the north is a turf rampart lying within the ditch, and apparently never completed. There are entrances in the middle of the east, west and south sides. The outer ditch cuts through the defences of Camp 2, lying to the east and enclosing 2 hectares. Polygonal in plan, Camp 2 has a V-shaped ditch 1.12 metres deep and 1.45 metres wide. Two gates on the east and one on the north-west are defended by a one sided out-turn rampart extension. Turf buildings have been found in the interior. 90 metres west is Camp 3, the most substantial earthwork, its ramparts still 3 metres above the ditch bottom. The camp is roughly square and covers 2.6 hectares, with rounded corners. The rampart of sand and rubble originally supported a wooden palisade. The earthwork had four entrances, one on each side, with turf buildings and a system of internal roads. Camp 4 lies immediately to the east of Camp 3 and its west ditch was filled in and overlaid by the ramparts of the former. It is similar in plan to Camp 3 but its area is slightly smaller, and its single bank and ditch are only half its scale. Its gates, one on the west and two on each of the north and south sides, are protected by inturn out-turn ramparts.

Excavations suggest that Camps 2 and 3 were coeval and were superseded by Camps 1 and 4. All date from the early second century.

The earthworks have been thought to be legionary practice camps, but Camp 1 may be a permanent fort on Wade's Causeway (North Yorkshire, 7), which passes through the site.

3. Goldsborough: signal station NZ 835152
The site is alongside the Goldsborough-Kettleness footpath leading north from Goldsborough at 836147.

The best-preserved of the Yorkshire signal stations built by Theodosius, Goldsborough was defended by a V-shaped ditch 3.7 metres wide and 1.2 metres deep, perhaps crossed by a wooden bridge. Inside the ditch are the foundations of a wall separated from the ditch by a 9.8 metres berm. The wall was 1.2 metres thick, enclosing an area 32 metres square. The wall angles were rounded, with semicircular projecting bastions for artillery. There was a 3 metres wide inturned entrance on the south side, with pivot stones for a double door. This gave access to an unpaved courtyard with a south-east well, 1.8 metres across and 2.6 metres deep. At the centre of the courtyard are the foundations of a tower 14 metres square with walls 1.5 metres thick, originally standing 27 to 30 metres high, and entered by a door aligned on the courtyard gate. In the south-east corner of the tower were the skeletons of two men and a large dog, which may be mute testimony to the end of the site early in the fifth century after perhaps twenty or thirty years of use. The site is now marked by a prominent mound and no stonework is visible as it was covered over after excavation.

4. Malton *Derventio*: fort   SE 791718

The site is a public open space on the outskirts of the town near the gasworks and the fire station.

There are few visible traces of the forts and large *vicus* of *Derventio*. The site was originally an 8.9 hectares camp used by the IX Legion. The first fort dates from AD 79, with turf ramparts and a single ditch. Portions of the ramparts, enclosing 3.2 hectares, are traceable on the north-east and south-east, as is the annexe which ran down to the river Derwent. The original turf ramparts were reinforced with stone in Trajan's time, and the ditches were restyled and doubled on three sides. The fort may have been damaged in the early third century but was reconstructed. In the fourth century *Derventio* housed a cavalry force co-operating with the coastal signal stations. The museum is now in the old town hall in the centre of Malton.

5. Scarborough: signal station   TA 052892

The site is on Castle Cliff but accessible only through Scarborough Castle, which is open at standard hours.

This is the only signal station on the Yorkshire coast where the plan can be clearly traced, although the east side of the structure has disappeared over the cliff. The turfed-over outline of the station has been marked out in concrete and shows the position of the square central tower defended by an outer wall with corner bastions. The surrounding ditch has been dug out on the south and west. The visible remains are partly obscured by a series of later medieval chapels. The station suffered a similar fate to the other Yorkshire sites at the end of the fourth century or later.

6. Stanwick: hillfort   NZ 180115

The site lies to the east and west of the B6274 and on either side of the Forcett-Aldbrough road.

This huge Brigantian earthwork, built and occupied during the Roman period, encloses 302 hectares. Excavations in 1951-2 suggested three phases in its evolution.

The first earthwork was The Tofts, a hillfort south of Stanwick church, enclosing 6.9 hectares. Only on the west side, in a plantation, can it be seen. It had a V-shaped ditch 5.5 metres wide and a bank, with a counterscarp bank on the north, and a stone-flanked entrance near the north-west corner, now obscured by the plantation wall. The Tofts is dated to the early first century AD, and circular huts inside the banks indicated permanent occupation.

In phase 2 the north side of the hillfort was levelled when it was incorporated into a large work, an enclosure of 53 hectares, north of The Tofts. This earthwork is mainly north of the Mary Wild

53. Wade's Causeway, North Yorkshire, on Wheeldale Moor.

Beck except where it joins on to the northern side of The Tofts. A gap in the south-east of this enclosure between The Tofts and Henah Hill was protected only by the brook. There was an entrance south of the western corner. The defences comprised a flat-bottomed ditch 4.9 metres deep and 12 metres wide and an earth and rubble bank faced with a drystone wall. A portion of this bank and ditch has been restored at a point 365 metres north of the Stanwick to Forcett road.

In phase 3, about AD 72, the fort had 243 hectares added when an area south of the Mary Wild Beck was enclosed by a ditch and bank, with an entrance on the south. The V-shaped ditch is inturned, slightly on the west and markedly on the east. It was never finished, because of some alarm, and the ditch was made continuous. Most of the circuit of the defences is visible from The Tofts.

Further excavations have cast doubt on this clear-cut sequence and shown that its interpretation is still far from clear. Romanised tableware and building materials were delivered to the site as early as the 40s (i.e. before the conquest of Britain had reached the north), doubtless to secure the allegiance of a member of the Brigantian royal family. One school of thought links the subsequent fortifications to the political convulsions in which Venutius deposed Queen Cartimandua, revolted against Rome in AD 69 and met his end at the hands of Petillius Cerialis' legions a few years later. Sceptics, however, stress the unsuitability of an unfinished 283 hectare enclosure as a rebel stronghold and the lack of evidence for Roman assault, preferring to place these historic events elsewhere.

7. Wade's Causeway: road   SE 805975
The best stretch is on Wheeldale Moor, near Goathland. It is signposted immediately east of the minor road leading south across the moors from Egton Bridge.

This 1.2 km stretch of road, perhaps the most spectacular exposed section in Britain, is maintained by English Heritage. Its present surface of rough slabs is due to the removal by weathering of the finer, upper layer of metalling. Drainage culverts with capstones *in situ* can be seen at intervals along its length.

8. York *Eboracum*: colonia and fort   SE 600520

Most of the visible remains of the Roman fortress and city of *Eboracum* date from the fourth century. The first fort, 20 hectares in extent, was founded in AD 71-2. It was rectangular, with rounded corners. Two of its main streets have their lines preserved by Stonegate and Petergate. The first ramparts were built in stiff clay in Agricola's time and were faced in turf with timber towers. In 107-8 stone wall gates and towers were added, and these were rebuilt under Severus, the new wall measuring 1.8 metres thick. Early in the fourth century the fort was remodelled and provided with six interval towers and two massive angle towers with polygonal fronts dominating the river Ouse. During the life of the fortress a large *vicus* grew up beside the main road on the western bank of the river. It was given the status of *colonia* under Severus and became the capital of *Britannia Inferior*. Two emperors held court and died here, Severus in 211 and Constantius in 306. There were probably large imperial palaces and other buildings.

The main visible remains are:

a. The Multangular Tower: this is the western angle tower of the fortress and is preserved in the Museum Gardens. It stands 5.8 metres high and is capped with medieval additions. Beside it is a stretch of fortress wall, 11 metres long, still standing 4 metres high.

b. The East Corner Tower stands behind the Merchant Taylors' Hall, Aldwark. It is best seen from the city wall (Monk Bar entrance). It consists of the remains of a rectangular internal tower still 2.7 metres high, with the curved face of the fortress wall 4.9 metres high in front of it. The fortress wall (with the medieval city wall above) is exposed from the eastern corner almost to Monk Bar, and the remains of an internal tower can also be seen along this stretch.

c. A further fragment of the fortress wall can be seen in the gardens in St Leonard's Place, almost opposite the theatre. Few buildings have been preserved within the fortress. Part of a fourth-century bath-house is preserved in the cellars of the Roman Bath inn in Church Street (landlord's permission required to visit). A column base is preserved under the Treasurer's House (National Trust), and a complete but broken column (probably part of the *principia*) has been re-erected upside down opposite the Minster.

d. A fine vaulted **sewer** over 46 metres long, with manholes, was discovered in 1972 at the corner of Swinegate and Church Street.

54. Plan of York showing the sites described in the text: a, The Multangular Tower; b, The East Corner Tower; c, St Leonard's Place; d, sewer; e, Minster.

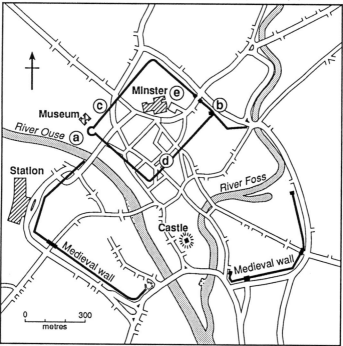

143

It is 1.2 to 1.5 metres high and is entered, appropriately, through a manhole. Arrangements to visit it must be made beforehand with the museum.

e. In the Minster part of the *principia*, found during the excavations to strengthen the Minster's fabric, can be seen *in situ* in the Undercroft. Most of the remains date from the fourth century and include several column bases (and the one re-erected outside). The excavations revealed that the columns were still standing in the ninth century. The remains are excellently displayed and fully labelled. One administrative room, a late addition to the rear of the complex, had decorated walls. Surviving fragments have been assembled to form one of the most superb examples of Roman painted plaster in Britain.

A wealth of material from Roman York is on display in the Yorkshire Museum, and there is a smaller collection in the Castle Museum.

YORKSHIRE: WEST

1. Ilkley *Olicana*: fort   SE 116478

The Roman fort of *Olicana*, 1.4 hectares in extent and now mainly covered by the church and the Manor House Museum, was originally an Agricolan foundation abandoned about 120 and reoccupied in the mid Antonine period. Its first rampart was of clay on stone foundations, with timber gates, and a wall was added under Severus. A stretch of the west wall can be seen exposed behind the museum and is 21 metres long and up to 1.2 metres high. The fort housed the second cohort of Lingones at the end of the second century. It continued in use and was rebuilt several times, lastly under Theodosius.

8. Roman sites in Wales

CLWYD

1. Ffrith: villa   SJ 286555
The site lies on the south-west side of Caergwrle.

A large number of rooms, which include a hypocaust, a room with an altar and store rooms, have been uncovered; they were of a civilian dwelling, probably the centre of an estate.

2. Pentre: villa   SJ 135759
The site is on the A548 1 km south-east of Flint.

Discoveries of stone foundations in 1978 were identified during subsequent excavations as a courtyard building with timber and clay constructed walls. Some fragments of painted wall plaster were recovered. Occupation material from the main part of the building ranged between *c.*120 and 140, while a hypocaust system (part of a bath wing) was not earlier than *c.* 200. Traces of lead working were found and dated to a later building phase. The villa site was in the vicinity of the Halkyn lead mines.

3. Prestatyn: forts and bath-house   SJ 062817
The site lies to the west of the A547 from Prestatyn to Meliden. The bath-house is in the cul-de-sac Melyd Avenue.

Rescue excavations on a new housing estate and near St Chad's School revealed traces of two successive forts. The ditch of one was 1.2 metres deep and 2.4 metres wide. No material later than *c.*150 was obtained. A bath-house excavated in 1936 and again in 1984-6 has been exposed and conserved. It has only three rooms, two of which were earlier than *c.*100, the cold room (with plunge-bath) being added *c.*150, implying that its predecessor was of timber. Some bricks were found to have been stamped by the XX Legion, indicating a connection with the legionary fort at Chester, Cheshire. Superimposed is an apparently post-Roman building.

The site has often been incorrectly identified as *Varis*, which is probably an unlocated fort near St Asaph.

4. Roman road

The A55 along the section from Ffrith-y-Garreg Wen near Holywell to St Asaph has been identified as a Roman road.

DYFED

1. Carmarthen *Moridunum*: town   SN 416202
The town stands where the A40 bridges the river Towy.

A Roman civilian settlement has been discovered beneath the town on the north-west of the site of the Norman castle, overlooking the bridge. The street system indicated the site of an early settlement. Excavations in areas of redevelopment have produced evidence of the town defences. These consisted of a rampart of turf and clay about 5.8 metres wide and 1.4 metres high. The outer ditch was 5.5 metres deep. This ditch was later filled in so that the foundation of the stone wall was laid in front of the rampart. This was 1.6 metres thick while the bank at the rear extended 17 metres. The earliest buildings were narrow strip buildings built of timber and dated to the second century. There were furnaces for iron and bronze working in these buildings on the north side of Priory Street. On the southern side there were foundations of masonry buildings for residents of the early fourth century. A large stone house succeeded these foundations.

An amphitheatre was discovered on the modern road to Lampeter. Excavations of the eastern entrance revealed the earth bank reinforced with timber. Traces of the timber steps set in the north bank were also detected but the timber seating has not survived. A drain was traced running down the bank and laid radially across the arena floor. The western bank of the oval structure has been laid out permanently and the arena wall reproduced in modern stonework.

2. Cwm Brwyn: fortified dwelling   SN 278150

The site is 17 km WSW of Carmarthen on the road to Laugharne and 5 km north-west of Laugharne church.

This is a long narrow building built of masonry with a flue and furnace at one end and standing inside a rampart and ditch which have survived on three sides. The building measured 29.7 by 7.6 metres. There might have been timber subsidiary buildings which would have formed part of an agricultural establishment.

3. Dolaucothi: gold mines   SN 665405

The A482 from Llandovery to Lampeter crosses the bridge at Pumpsaint; to reach the mines turn left and again left at the crossroads. Park by the Visitors' Centre.

Gold has been mined here possibly from late prehistory and certainly from the Roman period to the present day — each phase of activity disfiguring the evidence for its predecessor. The traditional Roman date of some features has been confirmed by radiocarbon dating of a fragmentary wooden waterwheel (now in the National Museum of Antiquities in Cardiff) and elucidated by fieldwork and excavation. Interpretation is based upon known Roman gold mines in Spain and elsewhere in the Empire; this, however, was probably the only such mine in Britain. Supervi-

55. Dolaucothi gold mines, Dyfed: the 'middle adit'.

sion and technical expertise were provided by the army, based on the fort at Pumpsaint (Dyfed, 6), and labour by civilians (whether free, conscripted or slaves is not known). It is possible, on overseas analogy, that by the end of the Roman period the mines

147

were managed by a civilian company for the government. There are traces of a workers' settlement, and the site of the pithead baths is known.

The gold-bearing ores were quarried both by opencast techniques and tunnelling. Placer deposits in the valley below may also have been exploited. One shaft, known as the 'Roman Lode', was 44 metres deep. Water was essential for prospecting (removal of overburden by *hushing*), quarrying (removal of loose debris) and washing the crushed ores. A Roman water-powered crushing mill is suspected, but not proved. The prominent stone Carreg Pumpsaint may have been originally used for crushing the ore by hand; it is more probably part of a post-Roman crushing mill, conceivably connected with the supposed (but undated) motte beside it. Three apparently Roman aqueducts can be traced as open channels along the valley side; one came from the river Cothi, another from the Annell and the third, taking a course between these two, came from Nant Dar along Bank Maes-yr-Haidd. One was 11 km long. Large embanked header tanks can still be found, originally with sluices to release water for hushing and other operations. The site of stepped washing tables has been provisionally identified. Since, however, medieval mining techniques varied little from the Roman, more than one period may be represented in the earthworks.

The mines are owned and managed by the National Trust, with the support of other bodies. The Roman features are not easy to identify, although rewarding to visit; a marked trail and guided tours start from the Visitors' Centre, where publications are available. Much of the machinery currently under restoration belongs to the equally interesting story of the abortive reopening of the mines in the 1930s. Although no longer producing gold commercially, the mines are proving a focus for research by archaeologists, geologists and students of mining technology alike.

4. Llandovery: fort   SN 770352

The fort stands around the small village of Llanfair-ar-y-bryn across the river from Llandovery and flanking the A483 on its course for Builth Wells.

The fort is about 2.3 hectares in area. Excavations across the defences in 1961-2 revealed four main periods of construction. The earliest were the earth and timber defences, together with timber buildings inside, which were associated with pre-Flavian sherds. It seemed that this fort was destroyed by fire. A second earth and timber rampart had been set on a raft of brushwood; this was probably the Flavian fort. The third defences of earth, revetted with stone, were constructed in the reign of Trajan.

Foundations of masonry buildings inside were of the main buildings.

The area of the fort was reduced by the construction of a slight bank and V-shaped ditch. This was dated to *c.*120-5. No occupation material later than *c.*160 was obtained.

Some of the Roman buildings were destroyed when the vicarage was constructed in the eighteenth century. The church is built inside the fort.

5. Llanio: fort   SN 644564
The site is on Llanio Isaf farm, where permission should be sought.

A rampart of turf and clay mixed with gravel proved to be 5.5 metres wide and was associated with an outer V-shaped ditch 3.4 metres wide and 1.2 metres deep. Excavations conducted within the rampart revealed the line of a street and the ends of timber buildings showing four periods of occupation.

A large building in the central area of the fort had been constructed on masonry foundations and had an external colonnade. This is believed to have been the *praetorium.* It was burnt at some time in its history. A ditch beneath the building had been filled in before its construction. The occupation material ranged in date from *c.* AD 75 to 120.

Observations in a sewer trench detected buildings, ovens, drains and iron slag which must have been part of an extramural settlement.

The fort is now invisible, but the remains of an excavated bathhouse can still be found (in poor condition).

6. Pumpsaint *Luentinum*: fort associated with Dolaucothi gold mines   SN 665405
The fort lies beneath the main A482 in the field south of the Dolaucothi Arms hotel.

The fort, discovered since the rescue excavations of 1972, was 2.3 hectares in area. A rampart of turf and clay had been built with two ditches beyond it. Trenches on the west and south showed a stone wall which was constructed across the site and which reduced the fort area to less than half its original size. Presumably the whole of the reduced fort was enclosed by a stone wall. The north gate was excavated; the original structure was erected in the Flavian period and continued in existence to the second century.

Seven buildings within the fort were explored. The occupation material ranged from *c.* AD 75 to 150. A section across the main north-south road showed that it had eleven surfaces. The earliest timber buildings were replaced by four others which appeared to have been used as workshops since there were six bowl furnaces constructed in them. Further exploration along the bank of the river Cothi produced foundations of timber buildings which may have been part of a civilian settlement. The name *Luentinum* probably refers to gold-washing.

7. Trawscoed: fort   SN 671172
The fort lies to the north of the B4340.

Excavations on the eastern side of the fort showed the defences to consist of a turf rampart 4.1 metres wide with a turf and clay revetment. Beyond were a berm and a ditch 3 metres wide and 0.9 metres deep. An early ditch had been filled in and the later rampart extended over it.

Part of a timber building in the *vicus* or settlement beyond the ramparts has been excavated. Ovens superimposed above each other, street surfaces and drains showed that they had been renewed at least three times. Occupation material extended to *c.* 120.

GLAMORGAN: MID

1. Gelligaer: fort   ST 133973
The fort lies beneath a field west of the church at Gelligaer on the B4254 north-west of Caerphilly. Permission should be sought from Gelligaer House.

Excavations in 1899-1901 exposed the masonry foundations of a complete fort with barrack blocks, granaries, workshops, administrative building and commandant's house, with the street plan of a textbook fort. It stood within masonry fortifications complete with angle towers and fortified entrances. It was a square fort 1.5 hectares. The rampart of earth, with stone revetment both inside and out, was 6 metres wide and can be seen in some of the field boundaries that enclose the site. There was no timber fort beneath the masonry. The date of the finds suggests that it existed during the fifth consulship of Trajan, that is *c.*103.

Exploration of the rectangular earthwork, traces of which can be seen east of the B4254, showed that it had been a Flavian predecessor of the stone fort. There is a theory that it was a marching camp or a temporary fort of the invasion period. The 2.4 hectares area of the camp was much larger than that of the stone fort.

Inscriptions that have survived from the gateways of the latter prove that it was occupied from the early second century until the later part of the same century. A study of the pottery has also demonstrated that the fort was reoccupied during the late third and fourth centuries.

There are indications that modifications were carried out on the site of the stone fort, as could be expected from continued occupation. When the outer fort ditches had been filled with a certain amount of soil and rubble an annexe was added to the south-east side of the fort. A stone wall 0.75 metres thick backed by an earth bank and with a ditch in front was joined on to the original fortifications. There was an entrance also on the south-east side. It contained some irregularly arranged buildings. In the north side of the annexe was a complete small bath building measuring about 43 metres. In the other half were rectangular buildings which might have been accommodation for travellers or official buildings. In date the annexe belongs to the period of fourth-century occupation.

A tile and mortarium kiln has been found near the fort; in the adjoining churchyard Roman burials and practice camps have also been found.

2. Penydarren: fort   SO 050068
The site is in Penydarren Park, north of Merthyr Tydfil.

Roman objects were discovered when Penydarren House was built in the eighteenth century but the site was not identified as a fort until excavations prior to the construction of a football ground were carried out in 1904. The exact size and plan of the fort can never be precisely identified because of the damage caused by the football ground. But one authority has suggested that it might have been square and of about 2 hectares and therefore could have accommodated one thousand infantry soldiers or five hundred cavalry. It was on the Roman road from Cardiff to Brecon.

Excavations in 1957 found the east rampart. It was built of solid clay with a rubble core set on a base of cobbles. In one section there was a turf revetment at the rear; in another trench the rampart was of clay, rubble and turves but no stone revetment has yet been found. Similar evidence has been found in trenches across the northern rampart. Therefore, though the finds indicate that the fort was in existence in *c.* AD 74, there does not seem to have been a rebuilding of the rampart as in other forts.

But though the rampart was not revetted there were stone buildings inside the fort and a granary over 20 metres long by 11 metres wide with buttresses and transverse sleeper walls. A well in the same area may indicate the courtyard of the administrative buildings. The 1957 excavations revealed timber buildings of two periods. The second phase had been constructed after those of the first phase had been burnt.

A bath building discovered early in the twentieth century outside the fort had the usual hypocaust rooms, a furnace and culvert. Burials, presumably from the sides of the roads leading out of the fort, have been discovered from time to time.

Studies of the pottery indicate that the fort was abandoned early in the reign of the Emperor Hadrian.

3. Ty Bryn: homestead   SS 916734

Occupation material ranging in date from the second to the third century AD has been discovered.

GLAMORGAN: SOUTH

1. Barry: building   ST 099664

The site is at Cold Knap, on the south-west edge of Barry. Access is from the A4050 via Salisbury Road (signposted Porthcerri and The Knap) and Romilly Road. Turn under the railway bridge and park at the end of Bron-y-Mor, by the Waters Edge hotel.

Excavated in 1980-1, this building, resembling a *mansio* (see examples at Wall (Staffordshire, 1) and (Chesterholm, Hadrian's Wall, 13), comprised 21 rooms on all sides of a courtyard, but no baths. An unusual feature is a cellar in the south-east corner. It was started in the late third century and apparently never finished. Its purpose is unknown; it might have formed part of an abortive project to link the fort at Cardiff with a new ferry service across the Severn estuary.

2. Cae Summerhouse: villa   SS 864779

The site is near the A48 between Cowbridge and Bridgend.

A rectangular enclosure shows a bank and ditch entered by an elongated funnel-shaped passage with sides that had been revetted. Beneath the Roman level there had been an iron age hut and a corn-drying kiln had been inserted into the end of a ditch.

Another enclosure, in the shape of the letter D, was bounded by a ditch 0.9 metres wide, which had been filled up, sealing occupation material of the first and second centuries. A drystone wall was built as a courtyard boundary over the filled ditch. One building of four-post construction was uncovered. This may have been an enclosure for stock associated with the main occupation site. The evidence of finds ranged from the late first century to the late fourth.

3. Cardiff: fort   ST 181788

The site lies north of the A48 within the site of the Norman and medieval castle, standing beside the main east-west road through the city.

It has long been established that the masonry at the base of the curtain wall of the present castle was the foundation of the fourth-century defences of a fort built on the coast to combat attackers from the Irish Sea. The Roman masonry is most clearly defined on the southern side, while the nineteenth-century restoration copied a typical fourth-century military gateway and towers in the rebuilt north and south gates. Some details, in particular the overall height, have been disputed. For similar reconstructions at Manchester and South Shields see Greater Manchester, 2, and Tyne and Wear, 1.

Excavations within the castle have discovered two timber forts, both of which have shown at least two periods of occupation.

Two timber buildings, possibly barrack blocks of the earliest fort, have been partially uncovered. Some of the sills of their foundations were removed and the void was filled with clay before the construction of the second fort. On the evidence of the 'Claudian copy' coinage, the first fort has been dated to the reign of Nero. It was defended by a ditch about 3 metres wide and 1.2 metres deep dug south of a rampart composed of laid turf.

Traces of the defences of the second fort have been uncovered east of the central axis and between 35 and 50 metres south of the north wall of the fourth-century fort. Part at least of this fort lay beyond the line of the wall. On the south side of the second fort a further rampart had been constructed on the line of the ditch of the earliest fort. A new ditch was dug beyond it.

An area of occupation dated to the second and third centuries lay outside the second fort; this may indicate a *vicus*.

Excavations in another large area within the site of the first fort showed traces of burning, proving site clearance with bonfires. The sloping ground had been deliberately levelled and the buildings were divided by cobbled streets flanked with gullies. In a higher level gullies associated with a deep level of humus correlated with the third and fourth centuries, which would be the period of the late fort. This activity had destroyed some of the levels below it.

4. Cowbridge *Bovium*: settlement SS 993747
The former course of the A48 passed from east to west through the medieval walled town. Today the bypass is to the north.

Some Roman finds had been made previously, but during the rescue excavations in 1976 near the modern town hall a Roman street with a ditch beside it was discovered. Foundations of rectangular buildings of both stone and timber were uncovered near it.

5. Ely: villa ST 146762
The site is 1.6 km south-east of Cardiff and south of the A48 as it passes out of the city to the west. The villa was found in the middle of the Ely racecourse and lies behind the Ely Eye Hospital.

The masonry foundations of a winged corridor house with courtyard walls forming a second wing were excavated. A considerable amount of ironworking had been conducted on the site in the functional section of the villa building. The main building was constructed in the first half of the second century. A verandah fronted the winged building. A complete set of baths was constructed at the end of this long hall in the side wing. The second structure was demolished and in the early fourth century the whole site was enclosed with earthworks which formed a protection from attack.

6. Llantwit Major: villa   SS 959699
The site is to the east of the B4265 from Llantwit Major to Wick; there are very slight surface indications in the field known as Caermead.

The complex buildings of the courtyard-type villa were enclosed by a low bank and shallow ditch with a 4.6 metres wide opening. There was a wing containing the normal domestic rooms with mosaic floors while another wing contained working floors and traces of ironworking. Yet another basilican-type building may have been the store rooms or the quarters of the working people on the farm. The dating evidence ranges from the mid second century to the late third century and, after rebuilding, continues to the early fourth century. The dramatic discovery of 41 human skeletons of both sexes and three horses, apparently the victims of attacks by sea marauders, showed that the site continued to be occupied after the demolition of the main house.

7. New Mill Farm: homestead or settlement   SS 915698
Occupation material ranging in date from the iron age to the second and third centuries AD was concentrated within an area 65 by 25 metres.

8. Whitton: villa   ST 081713
West of Cardiff, the road to St Lythans and Llancarvan from the A4050 (Cardiff to Barry) passes the site.

A complex of buildings was constructed within an enclosure bounded by a ditch. The range of rooms on the northern side showed two main building periods. The earlier dated from about 200; another building approximately 19 by 11 metres was erected towards the end of the third century or in the early fourth. They were quickly rebuilt with a cellar at one end and the foundations of a circular timber building at the other end. There were two houses, 13.6 metres and 13.7 metres in diameter, partially overlying each other. A granary measuring 5.3 metres long stood in the south-eastern corner of the courtyard, slightly north of a previous granary. A well filled with much vegetable matter had a circle of eight postholes, showing the posts inclining towards each other to form a shelter.

GLAMORGAN: WEST

1. Coelbren: fort   SN 859108

The site is 1.6 km south-east of Coelbren village and west of the road from Coelbren to Dyffryn Cellwen before it joins the A4109. It stands on the west of the very distinctive Neath valley and lies on the line of the Roman road from Neath to the Gaer at Brecon.

The fort stands at the junction of two small rivers and covers an area of 2.1 hectares. The profile of the ramparts and the sites of the north, south and east gates can be seen, with the lines of the roads leading out of them. An annexe of 1.4 hectares was added to the east of the fort. The rampart stands highest on the north side, where it is 6.1 metres wide and 0.61 metres high, and is built of turf and clay.

The excavations of 1904 on the fort defences showed that they were made of turf, clay and brushwood, were 7.3 metres wide and had a berm with two ditches beyond. At the corners and on the south side the rampart had been constructed on oak logs, brushwood or cobble. All the towers, gateways and the internal buildings were of timber. It is assumed that they were replacements of those of the Flavian fort since the occupation continued from the Flavian period until *c.*140-50.

2. Loughor *Leucarum*: fort   SS 564980

The fort lies on the south side of the A48 where the route crosses the river Dulais.

The Norman castle motte occupies the south-eastern corner of the Roman fort, whose rampart can be most clearly seen on the north side. A trench across the defences revealed a rampart of clay and turf set on a foundation of cobble, 0.9 metres wide and 1.2 metres high, fronted by a stone wall. The defensive ditch has been affected by later Norman work such as the insertion of a Norman angle tower into a partially filled ditch.

Limited excavations have uncovered two successive periods of construction. Granaries of timber were indicated, with sill beam slots which were 787 mm apart. The postholes and gullies were of the third period. A thick clay layer has been set over part of the filled-in ditch: this seems to have been done in the third century. The last period of occupation included a timber building of wattle and daub. Part of a bath-house had fragments of painted wall plaster in the debris of a channel.

3. Neath *Nidum*: fort   SS 7497

The A48 from Neath to Swansea passes over the fort diagonally.
The south-east and south-west gates were excavated when the
fort was discovered in 1949 and have been left exposed amid the
modern housing estate in, appropriately, 'Roman Way'.

Traces of the north-west defences were revealed by excavations in the playing field north-west of the main road. During
extensions to the grammar school the stone wall of the latest
rampart was discovered. The area of the fort was 2.4 hectares.

The earliest defences have not been discovered but a black
layer has been detected in each of the excavations undertaken on
the site. It is assumed that the earliest fort would be of the Flavian
period, when the site was cleared and the military forces were
first penetrating into the tribal area.

A clay rampart and ditch found in two separate excavations are
allocated to the second phase of the fort occupation and these are
dated to the *c.*80-5 Flavian period. A hiatus seems to have
occurred in the occupation of the site. The fort was reoccupied in
*c.*120-5 and the stone defences were erected. No Antonine pottery seems to have been found.

Though no military force may have been on the site, a *mansio*
may have continued in the third century. A milestone of the reign
of Diocletian proves the importance of the east to west road and
of the route from *Nidum* to Coelbren and to Brecon Gaer to the
north-west. *Nidum* stood at a strategic site at the estuary of the
river Neath.

GWENT

1. Abergavenny *Gobannium*: fort   SO 298141

The town is situated on the A40 from Monmouth to Brecon and on
the A4042 from Newport to the south.

Evidence obtained from several excavations has shown traces
of Roman military installations and later civilian occupation. A
rampart of turf and timber was discovered beneath a post-Roman
bank in the vicinity of the Norman castle. From the occupation
material obtained it was shown to have been in existence under
Nero. A trench on the line of Castle Street produced evidence of
wattle and daub buildings.

2. Caerleon *Isca Silurum*   ST 337907

The site is 5 km north-east of Newport and 2.4 km from the M4 on
the B4236.

The fort was the permanent base of the Second Augustan
Legion after the conquest of the Silures and the tribes in the west
by Julius Frontinus in AD 74-8. The first period defences were an

earth bank and ditch with timber buildings. An inscription dated to *c*.100 in the reign of Trajan indicates that some rebuilding in stone was carried out. Recent excavations have shown that not all the barrack blocks were replaced immediately in stone; further exploration beneath the stone foundations of the *principia* did not find evidence of an early timber structure. The emergency exploration in the central area of the fort showed the masonry *principia* to have measured 64 by 27 metres. The occupation material ceased after the third century, when the fort was abandoned.

Excavations of the area adjoining the Bull Inn car park have uncovered an impressive internal bath building. A bath building had previously been discovered outside the fort defences. The portico of the large *palaestra* has been found, associated with a series of hypocaust rooms and marble-stepped plunge baths. Now known as the Fortress Baths (to distinguish them from others partly uncovered on the west side of the amphitheatre) they are well displayed under a covered building and represent the most spectacular display of a legionary bath-house in Roman Britain. Visitors should combine this visit with the excellent new Legionary Museum nearby, beside the church.

From the museum a quiet road (signposted) leads to the north-west corner of the fort to see the defences and some of the pairs of

56. Caerleon, Gwent: the earthen seating banks of the amphitheatre.

57. *Caerleon, Gwent: the waiting room beneath the amphitheatre seating.*

barrack blocks are laid out with masonry. The area is entered by a path through the defences. Recent evidence has shown that the stone revetment was not added to the earth bank until *c.*120. A number of circular tile-built ovens can be seen in the tale of the internal bank beside the street built within the defences. The angle tower of the defences can be seen and near it the foundations of a latrine with its characteristic drainage system.

The barrack blocks, in two paired lines of double rooms, were set in such a way that two blocks confronted each other. The more spacious and elaborate rooms at the end of each block were for the centurion and his assistants. There were twelve double rooms set behind the colonnade along the front of the blocks.

Similar barrack blocks had been constructed throughout the greater part of the 20 hectares fort but these lie beneath the modern town. There was much rebuilding in the early third century but by the beginning of the fourth century the garrison had been moved. Before the end of the Roman authority in Britain the legion was at Richborough.

Situated outside the fort on the western side is the amphitheatre, in the guardianship of CADW (Welsh Historic Monuments). It was built *c.* AD 80 on the normal oval plan with passages dividing the segments of the earth bank, which were contained in stone walls. The seating would have been timber benches, which would have continued, except for narrow gangways, over the passages leading into the arena. On one side, beneath the seats reserved for the high-ranking officers, is a small room in which the gladiators and other performers would have waited their turn. There is a niche in the wall where an altar to the goddess Fortuna would have stood. Amphitheatres of this kind were used to demonstrate military tactics and strategy and for the commanding officer to address the soldiers, though there had been some modifications to its structure during the mid second century and again in the early third century.

An extensive native settlement with timber buildings stood between the fort and the river in the vicinity of the amphitheatre. The extramural bath buildings were also here. A visitor walking back from the site passes through the west gate of the fort, marked only by a plaque today, and continues along the line of the principal street towards the church, which stands on part of the *principia.*

A small classically styled building with portico and columns near the church is the Legionary Museum. The inscribed stones, including the one dedicated to Trajan in 100, have been set up. All the pottery, coins, fragments of equipment and other material normal for a military site are displayed. Cremation burials were discovered. A stone from the amphitheatre inscribed by one of the centuries which helped to construct it, the century of Rufinus, is on view. There are others in the building itself. The collection illustrates the typical conditions of life in a military garrison.

3. Caerwent *Venta Silurum*: town   ST 469905
8 km west of Chepstow the A48 from Newport bypasses the village, whose main street lies approximately on the east-west road of the Roman town.

Caerwent was the tribal capital of the Silures, a fact which is recorded on the pedestal of a dedication to Paulinus, who had commanded the II Legion and who later became governor of Narbonensis and Lugdunensis in Gaul. This stone, perhaps the base for a statue, was set up by decree of the local senate of the community of the Silures. This stone and another, which is dedicated to Mars Ocelus, can be seen in the church porch together with a few other finds from the site. The majority of the finds are at the Newport Museum, which is in John Frost Square in the centre of the modern shopping complex in Newport.

The town of 18 hectares is square in plan and before 130 a bank and ditch surrounded its perimeter, though the town must have been founded in the late first century. It is possible to walk round the stone walls, which were built in the late second or early third century. The polygonal bastions were added to increase the defences after 340. The south gate survives to the pillow or springer stones of the arch, and even one or two voussoir stones remain. The gate had been blocked up except for a drain at its base, presumably during the fourth century, when there was danger of attack from the coast. The north gate is partially visible behind the North Gate Hotel. The north and south gates were both of single gate type with flanking towers. Neither of the east or west gates has survived though part of the southern tower of the east gate can be seen. Since it is not bonded into the wall it may be earlier; as these gates were on the main street of the town they were probably built with dual arches.

The church stands south of the *forum* and *basilica*, but nothing of these foundations can now be seen. The baths, excavated in a field near the church, are no longer exposed. Extensive excavations were carried out and a large part of the town grid system and its buildings is known, but only a small temple of Romano-British type has been exposed adjoining a caravan site in the centre of the town east of the *forum* and *basilica*. It was built in the late third century and a long hall with an apse at one end was added in the fourth, with other ancillary rooms. Pagan worship evidently continued here while Christianity was the official religion.

To the west of the *basilica* and *forum* at Pound Lane some of

58. Caerwent, Gwent: the walls and added bastions.

the houses of the town can be visited. The area of gravel within the site and nearest to the modern east-west road indicates the surface of the Roman street. Two narrow shops extend from the street to include dwelling rooms at the back. They were built about 100. The eastern house was demolished in the second century and the surviving building was extended and had a courtyard. Occupation continued to the fourth century.

Recent excavations have revealed another bastion in the north-western corner. A section cut across the outer ditch has shown that it was 9.1 metres wide and only 1.8 to 3 metres deep; there was no dating evidence later than the fourth century in this excavation.

4. Caldicot: settlement   ST 473893
The site is 2 km south-west of Caerwent.

Rescue excavations prior to destruction uncovered an extensive area of shallow foundation trenches of circular hut floors and a working area divided by shallow boundary ditches. The occupation material showed that it had been inhabited during the iron age and the Roman period.

5. Hardnock Farm: homestead   SO 536152
This was a large complex building of the second and third centuries. Associated with it, evident traces of ironworking

proved that a part of the building had been used for industrial purposes. Bowl furnaces which were 305 mm in diameter and 165 mm deep were for bronze working. A second building had a hypocaust and evidence of painted wall plaster.

6. Usk *Burrium*: fort   SO 378006

The town stands on the A472 east of Pontypool and within 2.4 km of the A449 between Newport and Monmouth.

Extensive and complicated excavations during the late 1960s and 1970s have uncovered a fort of the Claudian period and another of the reign of Nero. Both were bases for campaigns by a force of the Second Augustan Legion among the local tribes. The river Usk provided an important route for the invading force. The low-lying site was subject to seasonal flooding and this may have strongly influenced the decision eventually to establish the permanent fort at Caerleon.

The Claudian fort was approximately 4 hectares in area. The defences were examined on the east and on the southern side. The rampart was 7.9 metres wide and the ditch 3 metres wide at the top. This fort preceded the Neronian defences, the rampart of which stood on ploughed soil which contained samian pottery of the reign of Nero. This fort was about 20 hectares in area. Part of the east-west road within this fort was cleared. Material from the timber buildings of barrack blocks and granaries indicated an occupation of *c.* AD 55-60.

Following the destruction of the Neronian buildings a fort with a Punic ditch was constructed. It produced dating evidence of the period *c.*66-70.

Exploration under the modern castle located uncovered colonnades along the *Via Principalis* and fenced compounds in the southern area of the fort. The principal buildings stood behind them on the south while there were indications of workshops, offices and stores on the north.

To the rear of the southern rampart there were five pairs of granaries. They measured 7.5 by 9 metres, constructed on foundations of postholes and beam slots. The granaries measured 13 by 30 metres. A timber building north of the granaries contained furnaces for ironworking.

Occupation of the military phases ended in *c.* AD 75 when the legion was established at Caerleon, but civilians continued to live on the site. Rubbish pits produced dating evidence. Industrial activity including iron smelting was conducted during the third and fourth centuries. Graves of civilians have been discovered along the main routes leaving the town. The civilian settlement seems to have comprised small ditched enclosures within which were timber buildings of rectangular plan.

GWYNEDD

1. Aberffraw: fort   SH 354689

The earth rampart was 0.6 metres high and 4.9 metres wide with an outer ditch which was 4 metres wide and 7 metres deep. Evidence of ironworking was found. The ditch was recut several times. Another bank of clay and rubble with a stone revetment has been found. This was 4 metres wide and had timber work on the outer face. The ditch dug in the first period was silted up and had to be recut; it was 3.8 metres wide and 1.1 metres deep, with a curved profile.

2. Brithdir: fort   SH 773188

NNW of Llanfachreth near Dolgellau, the fort lies in a field east of the village and north of the road to Caer Gai from Coed-ty-Glas.

The fort was constructed to guard the valley of the river Wnion. It also guards a side valley to Llanfachreth. The Roman road from Tomen-y-mur entered the fort from the north-west. The rampart has been much damaged by ploughing but faint traces remain and they are 4.6 metres wide. The fort measures about 54 metres square. An entrance can be detected in the centre of the south rampart.

Rescue excavations have produced evidence of iron age occupation of the site. One four-post hut was discovered. Ditches running east to west proved to be the defences of a Flavian fort which was replaced by the masonry fortlet set on a different alignment sometime during the reign of Trajan. A set of military baths was found outside the early fort, as was a timber structure, divided into four rooms, and which had two furnaces, smithing hearths and stone-lined pits which may have been associated with tanning. It suggests that a native settlement existed outside the fort, but no evidence later than the reign of Hadrian was obtained.

Extramural buildings and evidence for industrial activity have been uncovered; these extended to beyond the south-west angle of the fort and were on the south side of the Roman road.

3. Caer Gai: fort   SH 878315

The fort was constructed on a height near the south-west end of the lake at Bala. It is reached by a lane from the north side of the A494, 1.2 km north of Llanuwchllyn.

The fort is a square enclosure of 1.7 hectares and part of the masonry rampart can be seen in some of the field walls. Excavations in 1965 revealed a turf bank dated to *c.* AD 75-80. There were three phases of timber buildings within the fort. The third phase may be dated to 120-30 but there was a decline of occupation after 100.

Buildings associated with the fort have been detected to the south-west since the late nineteenth century. A soldier of the Cohors I Nerviorum set up a pedestal to Hercules, so at some time the fort was garrisoned by this regiment.

4. Caer Gybi: fort   SH 247826
The fort stands on a cliff in the northern part of Holyhead, around the church of St Cybi. The rebuilt south gate stands at the top of the hill.

The fort has only three sides; the fourth was open to the harbour. It was in reality a protected landing point. The church and churchyard, dedicated in the sixth century to St Cybi, stand inside the walls and have preserved them in an otherwise built-up area. An area of 0.4 hectares is known at the top but the full area cannot be measured. The west side is 76 metres, the north and south sides 48 and 41 metres. The walls are of rough stones set in a herringbone style, measure 1.7 metres thick and stand to a height of 4 metres. The north and the west sides are the best preserved. The rampart walk can be seen from the churchyard. Round towers stand at the corners of the right-angled plan. The tower on the north-west is the only survivor of completely Roman work. When excavated in 1952 it was seen to be of a partially hollow design. The gate in the south wall may be an original entrance but it has been repeatedly restored.

No evidence for dating has been found but the plan and structure of the defences are of the fourth-century style of the other coastal defensive forts such as Cardiff and those in the south-east of England. This naval station will have been linked to a series of signal towers. One has been excavated and conserved on Holyhead Mountain (Gwynedd, 13), where the fourth-century dating confirms that presumed for Caer Gybi.

5. Caerhun *Kanovium*: fort   SH 777705
To the east of the B5106 from Conwy south along the river valley, take the next turning after the side road to Rowen.

Excavations of 1926-9 exposed the plan of the earth and timber fort entirely except for the north-east corner, on which the church and churchyard still stand. Parts of the course of the rampart with fragments of its revetment in stone can be seen both in the wall round the churchyard and in the well-preserved section bisected by the lane. It is believed that the buildings were replaced with masonry structures during the second century. But coins and other evidence, including the milestone recording the name of the fort, prove that occupation continued until the fourth century.

Further exploration of the area between the fort and the river and elsewhere in the vicinity has revealed the existence of an extensive *vicus.* There were narrow strip buildings along the north and south roads leading out of the fort.

6. Caer Leb: enclosed hut circle   SH 473674
The site is 2.4 km WNW of the old church at Llandar, south of the road leading north-west from Bryn-Siencyn (A4080).

Double banks and ditches enclose a five-sided area, with an entrance in the middle of the east side. The banks were faced with stones and it is possible that water filled the ditches. Excavations in 1866 uncovered a rectangular building and a circular hut associated with occupation material of the third century AD.

7. Caer Metta: enclosed hut-group   SH 536650
This enclosed hut group has been excavated in recent years. There are both rectangular and circular huts. Hut 4, one of the rectangular huts, was completely cleared and a line of three postholes seemed to be a partition across the hut. A part of the inner hut wall was reddened by fire. A survey of the associated field systems covered an area of 4 hectares.

8. Caernarfon *Segontium*: fort   SH 482624
The Roman fort stands on the higher part of the modern town overlooking the river estuary and the Norman castle. The A4085 road to Beddgelert passes over the foundations of the south-east gate and across the fort, dividing the south-east corner, which has been excavated, from the area previously uncovered, part of which is laid out for visitors to see.

The site museum, standing beside the main road, contains the finds from the site as well as plans of all the buildings of the various periods. The fort, for an auxiliary regiment of one thousand men, some of whom were mounted as a cavalry force, was established *c.* AD 78-80. A trench dug across the defences on the south-east sector produced sherds of samian pottery in the silt of the ditch of the Flavian period. This was associated with a rampart of earth revetted with turf and timber and with a width of 6.1 metres at the base. The ditch was recut with a different profile *c.*100-20. The rebuilding of the fort took place at different times during the late second century, the north-west gate in *c.*155, the other gates, the stone wall and the internal buildings not being completed until the third century or even the early fourth. A bath building built over a street of the first period was never completed. There was extensive damage to the fort in the late second century and again in the first half of the fourth century but it was reconstructed and occupied until the withdrawal of troops under

59. Caernarfon, Gwynedd: the fourth-century barrack blocks.

Magnus Maximus in 383. Most of the Welsh forts had been abandoned by this date. There was some slight occupation in subsequent centuries but it was not of a military character.

An extensive native town flourished outside the fort. In 1959 a Mithraeum was excavated east of the fort. It had been built *c.* 200 and was used for approximately a century, during which it was twice renewed.

Behind the museum the visitor can see fourth-century barrack blocks laid out in the grass in the section between the north-east and north-west gates. The course of the rampart can be seen. The principal buildings of both the *praetorium* or commandant's house and the headquarters building or *principia* have the characteristic plan with rooms set around a courtyard. The administrative building has the usual rooms beyond the assembly hall and a strongroom built beneath the room that would have contained the regimental banners and battle honours. An inscription in the museum gives the First Cohort of Sunici from Germany as the regiment in the fort in the early third century. There is little evidence for other cohorts that served at *Segontium*. A long rectangular building of a *fabrica* or workshop is also visible. But a granary belongs to the second century.

The south-west gate can be seen by taking the path opposite the museum entrance. Nothing is visible of the Mithraeum or the considerable civilian settlement which grew up near the fort.

166

9. Caer-y-twr: drystone wall   SH 218830
The wall is 1.8 km west of Holyhead on the summit of Holyhead Mountain.

A drystone wall encloses an area of 6.9 hectares. There is an entrance on the north-east corner where the rampart curves inwards. On the northern side the rampart is 4 metres wide and 3 metres high with indications that there was a rampart walk. The steep slope of the natural ground makes a ditch unnecessary.

10. Cefn Graeanog: enclosed hut group   SH 455489
The site is 137 metres south-west of Cefn Graeanog.

Complete excavation of the enclosed hut group was carried out because of a threat to the site. Five periods of occupation were distinguished and a great deal of environmental evidence was obtained about the crops grown and the activities of the inhabitants.

The group of huts had been enclosed with a masonry wall. Three circular huts could be distinguished. The first period of occupation, dating to about the fourth century BC, was enclosed by an earthwork. The site had circular buildings in both the first and second periods. Field systems marked by lynchets have been distinguished: the crops grown included wheat, rye and oats. The number of dwellings was increased in the third and fourth periods after a hiatus in the continuous occupation of the site. During the third century the huts were enclosed with a masonry wall 0.9 metres wide and three domestic houses were in use. The number of buildings was reduced in the next phase and though ironworking was carried out on the site in the late fourth century there was a general air of dilapidation in the enclosure. The whole area reverted to woodland when the occupation ceased.

Many enclosed hut groups have been recorded in the highland area of Wales but few have been excavated with such precision.

11. Din Lligwy: enclosed hut group   SH 496862
The site is 1.2 km north-west of Llanallgo church, which stands at the junction of the A5025 and the A5108 north of Benllech.

An enclosure wall of limestone 1.2 to 1.5 metres thick forms an irregular pentagon with two circular and seven rectangular huts, covering 0.2 hectares. There is an entrance in the north-east wall which leads through a rectangular hut used as a guard-room. The walls of the individual dwellings survive in places to a height of 1.8 metres. From the results of the 1905 excavation it would appear that it was occupied in the fourth century AD. It is possible that there was a timber-constructed settlement before the stone buildings. 800 metres from this settlement there is another extensive native settlement which has not been explored. Another group of huts at Pant-y-Saer continued in existence to the sixth century.

12. Hen Waliau 'Old Walls': enclosure wall   SH 482624

140 metres west of the fort of Segontium visitors can walk down to the level of the A487/A499 as it enters Caernarfon from the south at sea level. Standing to a height of 5.8 metres, the wall of the rectangular Roman enclosure can be seen behind the Ministry of Health car park.

It is believed that the enclosure was built in the early third century, perhaps to enclose a stores depot. The strategic site of *Segontium* continued to be an important defence base against attacks from the sea in the fourth century, just as the forts of the Saxon Shore in the south-east of Britain were constructed as a protection against enemies who harried the coast.

13. Holyhead Mountain: hut circles and signal tower
SH 212820

The site is 3.6 km west of Holyhead on the south-west slope of Holyhead Mountain and 450 metres west of Caer-y-twr (Gwynedd, 9).

In 1865 over fifty huts were recorded in this large settlement of round huts extending over the slope of the mountain from Caer-y-twr, which is the stronghold at the highest part of the mountain. In spite of much destruction to a site that may once have extended over an area of 6 to 8 hectares, one group of fourteen huts survives and another of six huts in the fields to the north-east can be visited. Some of the huts have internal features such as central stones and slabs of stone to define internal benches. In one of the rectangular huts copper slag was found, which may indicate a bronze worker's hut.

Evidence from stratified deposits within the huts on this and other sites in Gwynedd is plentiful and there is no doubt that occupation may have continued on some sites from the bronze age into the Roman period. Evidence from sites such as Cefn Graeanog, which has been scientifically excavated, has shown continuous occupation with only one hiatus throughout five phases.

On the very summit, beside the Ordnance Survey triangulation point, can now be seen one of the fourth-century signal towers that served, for instance, the naval station of Caer Gybi (Gwynedd, 4). Two walls of a tower 5.45 metres square are marked in the grass. To the north, the site of the next in the series can be seen on the summit of Carmel Head (SH 293424). This one is unexcavated.

14. Tomen-y-mur: fort   SH 707388

The fort is 4 km north of Trawsfynydd village. It can be reached

by a road to the east of the A487 Caernarfon to Dolgellau road.
The turning is south of the A470 to Blaenau Ffestiniog.

The site of the fort commands wide views of the Ffestiniog valley and is 275 metres above sea level. There is a complex of sites including the fort, in the north-west bank of which a large Norman motte has been constructed. To the east of the fort is the earth bank of an oval amphitheatre. 90 metres beyond the north-west gate of the main fort is a small practice camp. On the south-east of this is another possible practice camp. A bath building was excavated between the fort and the river on the south-east: these are now merely grass-covered irregular mounds. A high embankment leading to the river was on the line of the road that led south to Caer Gai. A large marshy rectangular area to the east has been described as a parade ground.

The first fort was 1.7 hectares and would have accommodated a garrison of a thousand soldiers. The fort was reduced in area to 1.3 hectares by another rampart and ditch which were constructed across the area within the fort on the north-west. Excavations in 1962 showed that the first defences were constructed of earth on a turf foundation with a timber palisade above. A counterscarp was noticed beyond the two defensive ditches, which were later replaced by a single ditch. Only very slight evidence of dating survives for the stone-revetted rampart constructed across the Roman street which had been laid out behind the main buildings of the early fort. It does not seem that the principal buildings were rebuilt in stone. No occupation material later than *c.*140 has been found.

Inscriptions from Tomen-y-mur are in the Segontium Museum.

POWYS

1. Brecon Gaer *Cicucium*: fort   SO 002297

The site is 5 km west of Brecon on the A40. It is best to take the minor road from Brecon to Battle and, turning left at Cradoc at a crossroads, it is necessary to turn right to Y Gaer farm, where permission must be sought to visit the site.

The fort, constructed at the confluence of the river Yscir with the Usk, is important as it was at the junction of many important roads. The road from Caerleon came up the Usk valley and continued from this point to Llandovery and Carmarthen and the west of the territory. Another road came from the forts in the Neath valley and continued north to Castell Collen. A short distance from the site a road led to Gelligaer and Cardiff. For the best of these roads, see Sarn Helen (Powys, 5). It is not surprising that the Gaer was one of the largest auxiliary forts in Wales. An inscription on a tombstone found outside the fort records that the cavalry unit of the *Ala Hispanorum Civium Romanorum* was stationed there soon after the construction of the fort, *c.*75-80.

Excavations in 1924-5 revealed a fort of 3.1 hectares defended by an earth rampart and two outer ditches. In *c.*140 a stone wall was built and the west gate had elaborate square guard chambers which extended out in front of the fort wall. The principal buildings in the centre of the garrison were rebuilt in stone though the *principia* had two distinctive differences from the more usual plan: a long narrow room was added on the north side and a covered hall extended over the north-south street passing in front of it. The comandant's house extends over the street parallel with the main east-west street behind the complex. Evidence that two timber building periods had preceded the stone structure came from beneath the house. It is possible that the extension across the space in front of it and the covered hall of the *principia* may have been additions. There is no evidence that the barrack blocks were ever rebuilt in stone. A small bath building constructed in the front part of the fort and on a different alignment is a later intrusion. It must have been constructed when the number of cavalry soldiers was reduced or in the fourth century when there might have been only a holding force. Visitors to the fort can inspect the rampart and main gateways but none of the main buildings is visible.

Evidence of a large civil settlement was obtained in the excavations of the 1920s. It extends to about 275 metres beyond the north gate. One shop was of masonry though most of the buildings were of timber. Another stone building to the west may have been a *mansio* or a station for the imperial post.

The date for the end of the fort's history is not precise. The stonework was rebuilt once after the original construction. The regular garrison had been removed in the second century though a smaller force reoccupied it in the late third century.

2. Caersws: Roman forts

Two Roman forts have been discovered near modern Caersws.

a. Caersws I   SO 041926

Detected on an air photograph, it stands 1.2 km east of the modern village, standing on a spur and overlooking the river Severn south-west of Llwyn-y-brain farm.

Three parallel ditches are the clearest surface indications of what can be seen on the air photograph. These are the defences on the south-east of the fort. It seems that the fort covered 3.8 hectares, with sides measuring about 219 by 170 metres. It has been deduced that it is pre-Flavian in date and was one of the advance bases for the campaigns from Wroxeter which marked the early penetration of the Roman army into Wales.

b. Caersws II   SO 029920
*The fort stands near Pentre Farm. The A489 Newtown to
Machynlleth road passes over the north-east corner of the fort.
The south-west corner was damaged by the construction of the
railway in the nineteenth century. The external bath building was
buried beneath the railway goods yard.*

The fort covers an area of 3.1 hectares and is of great importance as the hub of several Roman roads linking a number of
centres. It is connected with Wroxeter to the east, with Brecon
Gaer to the south, with Caerhun to the north and the forts in
Gwynedd to the north-west. It stands near the confluence of the
river Severn with its tributary the Carno.

Excavations were carried out in the early twentieth century.
The evidence from them was studied and published from the
1930s to the 1950s but the most recent excavations of 1966-7
provided the clearest evidence for the history of the site. The first
defence system was a rampart of clay with a revetment of turf in
front and a ditch 4.1 metres wide. The upper part of the rampart
was slighted and the ditch partly filled in. In the second period
the rampart was made higher, the ditch was filled with stone and
a new rampart face, bonded into the earlier work, was extended
over the ditch. In the last period the rampart was faced with stone.

There were timber buildings within the fort which were linked
with two separate periods of early, even pre-Flavian pottery.
There was evidence of deliberate demolition. From the pottery,
this appears to have been at some time in the late first century.
Another timber period showed marked improvement of construction. In the third period the barrack blocks continued to be of
timber though the main buildings were constructed in stone. The
rear portion of the fort was dismantled but third- and fourth-
century pottery proved continued occupation.

Excavation trenches were also cut outside the fort and produced evidence for timber storehouses of the Flavian period.
Further trenching indicated foundations of buildings of a civilian
settlement outside the fort. The defences are most clearly seen at
the south-west corner by the station and the level-crossing.

3. Carno: temporary camp   SN 962966
*The camp stands in a field called Caer Noddfa, north-west of
Caersws on the flood plain of the Carno. The A470 passes beside
the site, which lies next to Carno church.*

The fort has an area of 0.9 hectares. The ramparts are only
faintly marked and parts are under the farm on the south corner.
A turf rampart 4.3 metres wide was associated with a V-shaped

ditch 3.4 metres wide and 2 metres deep. No finds were made. Part of the rampart in the north corner was damaged when the Knights Hospitaller of St John built their hospice there in the thirteenth century. The name of the field, Caer Noddfa or the Field of Refuge, is a reference to this hospice. The inn across the road from the site is called the 'Alepo Traveller'.

4. Castell Collen: fort   SO 055628

The fort stands overlooking the river Ithon, north of Llandrindod. It is reached by turning to the right after crossing the river from the A4081 (Llandrindod to Rhayader). The road leads to a farmhouse and the fort stands behind it.

The banks and ditches of a square fort can be seen together with an isolated bank and ditch lying to the west, nearer the farmhouse. The area of the complete square fort is 1.5 hectares. It was therefore large enough to hold a garrison of five hundred men. The detached rampart was once thought to have been the vestiges of an annexe but excavations have proved that it is the surviving part of the first fort of 2 hectares, which could have accommodated a force of one thousand men. This was defended with an earth bank and ditch and was built in *c.* AD 75-8. These defences were revetted in stone in the mid second century according to excavations carried out in 1954-7. The gateways were built with projecting semicircular gate towers. The stone *principia*, *praetorium* and granaries were exposed after the earlier excavations.

The rear area of the fort was abandoned at the end of the second century or in the early third century. A rear gate with a single entrance was built into the plan of the new square fort. The original central principal buildings were incorporated into the new fort plan. During the late third or fourth centuries the defences of the fort were completely rebuilt. There were intervals of complete decay and abandonment between these four main phases. The evidence from several trenches failed to find masonry barrack blocks but two periods were detected in the timber structures.

A bath building was discovered outside the fort to the south. This had many structural alterations. The undressing hall was very large and the latrine exceptionally long.

The defences can be traced throughout their length, with an unexplained extra bank and ditch to the west. Masonry of the *principia*, a granary next to it and the commandant's house to the south can still be traced in the centre of the site. They were excavated in 1911-13.

5. Sarn Helen: road   SO 969265

From Brecon, take the A40 (T), forking left at SO 030285 on to a minor road. After 7 km, look for the sign to the Mountain Centre and take the lane to the right. Park after about 200 metres.

This military road linking the forts of Brecon Gaer (Powys, 1) and Neath (West Glamorgan, 3) is at its best where it crosses the bleak and windswept heights of Mynydd Illtyd. To the north-east it is a green lane between modern stone walls, leading down to a farm. To the south-west it is an irregular causeway with quarrying depressions on either side. Large kerbstones can be seen beside the present track at the crossing of a stream on the lower ground. Beyond this, through the valley to the Camlais brook there is very little sign, though intensive fieldwork has excavated and recorded the causeway with cambered metalling and side quarries.

The name (shared with other Welsh roads) comes from a popular romance in the *Mabinogion,* 'The Dream of Maxen Wledig', in which Magnus Maximus gives his British wife, Elen Lyddawc, three fortresses in Wales connected by roads.

6. Y Pigwn: temporary camps   SO 827313

Take the A40 (T) west from Trecastle. After 7 km, take an unposted turning on the left just before the Halfway Inn (SO 832328). Take the car up the lane (sharp left at the 'No Through Road' sign) and park by the farm Hafod-Fawr. The lane continues to the site.

The Roman road westwards from Brecon Gaer (Powys, 1) clips the superimposed camps. The loop in the lane is often mistaken for the road, whose true course can be seen looking back from the crest — first a cutting at the crest, then a narrow *agger* down the hillside with a zig-zag at the steepest point. Post-Roman lead-mining has disfigured the south side of the site, but the road probably effaced one corner of the larger camp on which it was aligned.

Both camps belong to the campaigns of AD 47-78 and are fine specimens, one within the other at different angles. They were superseded by a permanent fortlet 450 metres to the west, which today is virtually invisible.

9. Roman sites in Scotland

THE ANTONINE WALL

The Antonine Wall was commissioned by Hadrian's successor, Antoninus Pius, as a response to unrest in southern Scotland in 139. Hadrian's Wall was evacuated and a new line chosen, from the Forth to the Clyde, a distance of 64 km. This wall was of turf — a material that is more durable than it might seem. It had a ditch in front 12 metres wide and 3.7 metres deep, and a military road behind it. In its final form it contrasted with Hadrian's Wall in not having milecastles and turrets — merely eighteen or nineteen forts at intervals of about 3 km (sixteen are known so far). This series evolved in two phases, and in addition six fortlets (for signalling) are known. The wall was probably begun in 142 and completed in 145. After about thirteen years a further revolt resulted in its temporary abandonment. A year later (or possibly less) it was reinstated, and it seems to have lasted until about 164, when the frontier was once again withdrawn to Hadrian's line.

a. Cramond   NT 190776
  North of the church, and accessible by the drive to Cramond House, the internal buildings of the fort have been excavated and marked out. This was a supply base for the wall, subsequently refurbished for Severus' campaigns in Scotland.

b. Kinneil Estate, Bo'ness   NS 984805
  A small fortlet with an adjacent stretch of the Antonine Wall rampart 550 metres west of Kinneil House has been excavated and displayed for visitors in the grounds of the Kinneil Estate, which is a public park. Descriptions and finds are displayed in the nearby Kinneil Museum.

c. Watling Lodge   NS 865798
  Although all traces of the Wall have disappeared, this is the most impressive section of the ditch, which here survives to roughly its original dimensions, about 12 metres wide and 4.6 metres deep. Between here and Bonnybridge the Wall itself is visible, with a beacon mound attached to its rear at NS 855798.

d. Rough Castle   NS 843798
  Although only 0.4 hectares in size, this tiny fort is very well preserved, with the stone foundations of some of the internal buildings still visible. A most unusual feature is the excavated and preserved *lilia* outside the north ditch; these are pits arranged

60. The Antonine Wall: the ditch at Watling Lodge.

in staggered rows, each originally with a sharpened stake in the bottom and camouflaged with vegetation.

175

61. The Antonine Wall: the 'lilia' at Rough Castle.

d. Croy Hill
NS 739760

The ditch is particularly well preserved here, for about 2.4 hectares, and in places the upcast mound in front can be discerned. The spectacular view to the north emphasises the skilful and commanding choice of line for the frontier. On the west brow of the hill are the faint traces of two beacon platforms, and for a short stretch the ditch was left undug as it had to be hewn from solid rock.

e. Bar Hill
NS 707759

This fort was 1.5 hectares in extent and was set a little way to the rear of the Wall — an unusual feature. The ramparts can be easily made out, and two of the internal buildings have been conserved for display; these are the well-preserved *principia* and the more fragmentary elongated bath-house. On excavation the well in the courtyard of the *principia* contained clear evidence of systematic demolition of the fort when it was excavated. A granary, workshop and timber barracks were also excavated in 1902 but are not now visible.

f. Bearsden
NS 525721

The bath-house of the fort comprises the best display of masonry remains on the Antonine Wall. It is roughly cruciform in plan, and most unusually the *apodyterium* and *frigidarium* were of timber — like the other fort buildings. The two *tepidaria* and the *caldarium* are especially well preserved, in stone, and military tastes were served by the inclusion of a *laconicum*. The rest of the fort is now under modern houses.

OTHER SITES IN SCOTLAND

1. Ardoch: fort   NN 840100

Take the A822 to Braco. Park at the north end of the village and cross the river bridge on foot. This is private land, and permission should be obtained from Keir Estate Office, The Mill, Station Road, Bridge of Allan, Stirling FK9 4JS.

The impressive visible remains belong to the later second century — the Antonine successor to an Agricolan fort. The multiple earthworks are finest on the eastern side; at the north-east corner, the slight outermost bank may be medieval (like the remains of a chapel in the centre of the fort) and the two outermost ditches (with bank) are possibly Agricolan. The irregular spacing of the northern defences betrays a reduction of the fort from 3.6 to 2.3 hectares, both phases being Antonine; the three outermost ditches, with remains of corners at north-west and north-east, belong to the larger fort. Two later ditches cross the space between these and the main inner rampart, which originally had a stone facing. Internal buildings of masonry have been excavated but are not visible. The fort was built for a mixed garrison of auxiliaries and legionaries.

To the north and north-east are very faint traces of a large annexe with a watchtower and no less than six overlapping marching camps — a complex covering the first to third centuries. The chronology is still disputed, and the traces are difficult to follow on the ground.

2. Bothwellhaugh: fort and bath-house   NS 730577

From the M74 take either the A723 to Motherwell or the A725 to Bothwell. The Strathclyde Country Park is signposted, and the car park is a picnic area beyond the river and the so-called 'Roman Bridge'.

This small 1.6 hectare fort was built in the late second century and despite modifications lasted little more than 25 years. Only the south-east rampart can now be traced. The adjacent baths were excavated in 1975-6 when the site was flooded to form a reservoir. They have been rebuilt on a new site nearby.

3. Burnswark: hillfort and Roman practice camps
NY 185787

Take the B725 from Ecclefechan; cross the railway bridge and keep straight on along a minor road which becomes a track.

177

On the hill to the north are the very faint traces of an iron age hillfort that was abandoned long before Roman times.

To the south lies a well-preserved, roughly rectangular Roman camp with an earlier fortlet incorporated into its north-east corner. The east, west and south gates are protected by *titula* and three gaps in the north rampart give access to three prominent mounds (known locally as the Three Brethren) facing the three former gateways of the hillfort. These were artillery platforms, and both stone *ballista* balls and lead sling bolts found on the hillfort were once thought to be evidence for actual assault on the native defenders. Excavation has since proved that the hillfort was deserted and that the Roman camp was built as a semi-permanent training ground.

From the hilltop, especially from a small Civil War observation post at the south-west end of the hillfort, can be seen the elongated outline of a second Roman camp to the north. One entrance is guarded by a *clavicula* and the rampart on the north side appears to be unfinished — both features suggesting another training exercise.

4. Castle Greg: fortlet   NT 050952
The site is 5 km south-east of West Calder on the east side of the B7008 north of its junction with the A70. It is about five minutes' walk from the road.

This tiny fortlet, a mere 45 by 55 metres, with a single bank and double ditch, is beautifully preserved. The single entrance is to the east.

5. Parkneuk: watchtower   NN 916184
Take the B8062 northwards from Kinkell Bridge. The site is in woodland on the right-hand side.

This tiny earthwork originally held a timber tower about 3.5 metres square in the centre. Around its base was a rampart of earth and turf about 3 metres wide, and a penannular ditch about 3.4-3.7 metres wide and 0.9 metres deep. The upcast from the ditch formed a low outer bank. Access was by a causeway through the banks and across the ditch, on the north side; this led for some 9 metres to an east-west road, now represented by a cleared strip in the wood.

This was one of a chain of at least eleven watchtowers (the 'Gask Ridge series') connected by road; they probably formed a temporary frontier under Agricola in the 80s. Clearly not a barrier, they were a means of observing people and controlling their movement. Parkneuk is the best-preserved of the series, most of which are now hard to trace. A second good specimen is at Muir o' Fauld (NN 981189), a third at Kaims Castle (NN 861129).

62. Parkneuk

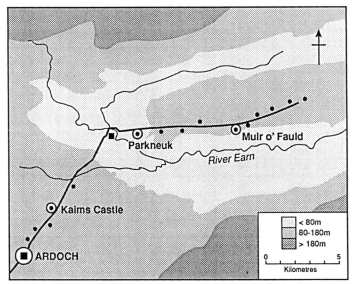

63. Watchtowers of the 'Gask Ridge series' (after D. Breeze).

6. Raedykes: temporary camp — NO 842902

Follow the A957 from Stonehaven and turn right at the first minor road signposted Stonehaven Riding School. Fork right almost immediately along the road which becomes a track. Park by the entrance to Broomhill Cottage.

This 38 hectares camp probably belongs to the 45 hectares Agricolan series. The outline is irregular, following the terrain, and much is obscured by gorse and bracken. The north and east sides have higher ramparts, and excavations have shown that this was deliberate, to compensate for the less steeply sloping approaches.

7. Woden Law and Pennymuir: hillfort and temporary camps — NT 768125 and 754140

Take the A68 across the border from England and turn right towards Edgerston Tofts and Hownam. At the crossroads 6 km on take the road signposted to Hownam and Hindhope. Park at the T junction by the derelict cottage of Pennymuir to visit the camps. Woden Law can be seen a mile or so to the south-east; to reach it, drive back to the crossroads and park, taking the path that represents the line of Dere Street. Turn right at the top of the hill.

At Pennymuir, the most prominent earthworks are those of an 18 hectares camp with a much smaller one in its south-east corner. The gates of both are defended by *titula*, most clearly seen on the north and east sides. The larger camp is undated but is probably a marching camp of double legion size. The smaller may have accommodated troops on manoeuvres at Woden Law. At Pennymuir a third parallelogram-shaped camp can be made out to the north-east of the others, and to the south of it a mere corner of yet another. Dere Street runs through this group of camps, crosses a small brook and climbs the northern slopes of Woden Law.

The hillfort has multiple ramparts that range in date from pre-Roman to post-Roman. Of particular interest are a semicircular outer earthwork running parallel to the oval hillfort and equidistant from it, and two linear features leading south from it with a cross-dyke, forming a rough letter A. Excavation has shown that these are Roman in date and, in spite of their tactical uselessness, were recut and therefore used more than once — presumably as training exercises; the semicircular bank was flat-topped and built on stone foundations, to take heavy artillery in a practice siege. When these were constructed the hillfort was unoccupied and the ramparts had already been slighted.

10. Roman sites in the Channel Islands

ALDERNEY

1. The Nunnery (Les Murs de Bas, Le Fort des Murs)

WA 59510813

The fort stands at the western side of Longis Bay. It is privately leased from the States of Alderney, and the interior is not accessible to visitors.

This little fort is traditionally a Roman building, much modified. Its documentary history begins in 1435, but the curtain wall and (originally) four semicircular shallow bastions are much earlier. The south-east portion has collapsed on to the beach, where the unaltered masonry of a bastion may be studied. Roman bricks are certainly used, or reused, in its masonry, whose largely undressed stone contrasts with the ashlar of the other island forts of Norman and later date. Its plan, with rounded corner, resembles that of the Yorkshire signal stations but it is much larger, and only excavation can establish the former existence of a central tower. Its position near sea level is less appropriate than Essex Hill nearby. In the absence, however, of proof to the contrary it is generally regarded as an element in the system of the *Tractus Armoricanus*, the Armorican counterpart of the Saxon Shore of Britain and eastern Gaul.

There is now nothing to be seen of the extensive Roman settlement nearby, on Longis Common, where pottery, burials and substantial buildings have been recorded. Finds from a rubbish pit of the late second century, excavated in 1889, are displayed in the museum in St Annes.

JERSEY

1. The Pinnacle: temple

54495547

Take the B35 to Le Puleq, where it doubles back and climbs steeply up the hillside to Mont de Vallet. Here take the B55 to Ville la Bas for about 600 metres and at the crossroads take the road to the left towards the cliffs. 23 metres further on, the road branches and the track to the left leads to the crest overlooking the Pinnacle Rock.

The spectacular Pinnacle Rock is separated from the mainland by a land bridge that bears two lines of prehistoric 'ramparts'. In front of it are the concentric rectangular foundations of a small building. Excavations between 1930 and 1936 proved it to be Roman on the evidence of Roman pottery and a coin of Commodus (180-91). It is the only unquestionably Roman building to be seen in the Channel Islands. At the time of excavation it was suggested that it might be an isolated signal station, but the excavators were probably right in identifying it as a temple of Romano-Celtic type. The identification is supported by the proximity of a spring, whose spirit might have been venerated, and by the very isolation of the site; the theory is weakened by the complete absence of dedicatory offerings, despite meticulous excavation. The restored foundations have been much disturbed in recent years.

64. Jersey, Channel Islands: the Roman temple at The Pinnacle, as excavated.

Further reading

Specialised works (paperbacks asterisked)

Nearly all aspects of Roman Britain are covered, subject by subject, in the comprehensive Shire Archaeology series. Each book has its own specialised booklist.

Some additional titles might be of interest: L. Allason-Jones *Women in Roman Britain* (British Museum Publications, 1989)* surveys a somewhat neglected topic; anyone studying mosaics and wall-paintings should try to obtain J. Liversidge *Furniture in Roman Britain* (Tiranti, 1955)* and those who wish to read the literary and other sources in translation should turn to S. Ireland *Roman Britain: a Sourcebook* (Croom Helm, 1986).

Three early historical episodes are separately studied by G. Webster, *The Roman Invasion of Britain, Rome against Caratacus* and *Boudica* (Batsford, 1980, 1981 and 1978), and the transition from later Roman Britain to early Saxon England by S. Johnson *Later Roman Britain* (Routledge, 1980). For topography (and introductory essays) the Ordnance Survey's *Map of Roman Britain* (fourth edition 1978) is indispensable.

General works (paperbacks asterisked)

The picture of Roman Britain has changed so rapidly in recent years that many of the older classics are sadly out of date. Some, such as J. Liversidge *Britain in the Roman Empire* (Routledge, 1968), can still be used with profit. Two magisterial works, moreover, continue to dominate the field: S. S. Frere *Britannia* (revised edition 1978, Routledge) and P. Salway *Roman Britain* (Oxford, 1981). Some stimulating ideas on economy and society have recently been advanced by M. Millett in *The Romanization of Britain: an Essay in Archaeological Interpretation* (Cambridge, 1990), and the latest synthesis is T. W. Potter and C. Johns *Roman Britain* (British Museum Publications, 1992). The latter has joined the earlier introductory booklet, also by T. W. Potter: *Roman Britain* (British Museum Publications, 1983*) which is still in print. For many, the most thoughtful (and inexpensive) general introduction is still M. Todd *Roman Britain* (second edition 1985, Fontana*).

Journals

Roman Britain has its own journal, *Britannia*, which includes an annual summary of excavations and new inscriptions and has generated its own monograph series. Its Empire-wide counterpart is the *Journal of Roman Archaeology*, while the literary and historical aspects of the Roman world are covered by the *Journal of Roman Studies*. Readers avid for up-to-the-minute information should subscribe to the bi-monthly *Current Archaeology*.

Maps

These maps show the locations of the sites described in this book.

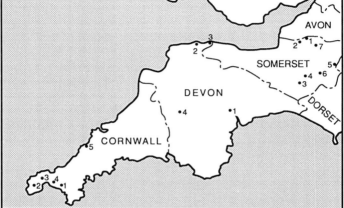

MAP 1.
Cornwall: 1 Breage; 2 Carn Euny; 3 Chysauster; 4 St Hilary; 5 Trevelgue Head.
Devon: 1 Exeter; 2 Martinhoe; 3 Old Burrow; 4 Sourton. *Somerset*: 1 Charterhouse-on-Mendip; 2 Cheddar Caves; 3 Ham Hill; 4 Ilchester; 5 Pen Pits; 6 South Cadbury; 7 Wookey Hole Caves.

MAP 2. (Opposite).
Avon: 1 Bath; 2 Keynsham; 3 Kings Weston; 4 Sea Mills. *Berkshire*: 1 Knighton Bushes; 2 Lowbury Hill. *Buckinghamshire*: 1 Bancroft; 2 Thornborough Mounds. *Dorset*: 1 Ackling Dyke; 2 Badbury Rings; 3 Cerne Giant; 4 Combs Ditch; 5 Dorchester; 6 Hod Hill; 7 Jordon Hill; 8 Kingston Down; 9 Maiden Castle; 10 Stinsford; 11 Woodcuts. *Gloucestershire*: 1 Bury Hill Camp; 2 Chedworth; 3 Cirencester; 4 Gloucester; 5 Great Witcombe; 6 Littledean; 7 Lydney Park; 8 Spoonley Wood; 9 Wadfield. *Hampshire*: 1 Alice Holt Forest; 2 Bitterne; 3 Bokerly Dyke; 4 Farley Mount; 5 Portchester; 6 Portway; 7 Rockbourne; 8 Silchester; 9 Winchester. *Hereford and Worcester*: 1 Kenchester. *Isle of Wight*: 1 Brading; 2 Brading Down; 3,4 Carisbrooke; 5 Newport. *Leicestershire*: 1 Great Casterton; 2 Leicester; 3 The Raw Dykes. *Northamptonshire*; 1 Irchester; 2 Towcester. *Oxfordshire*: 1 Alchester; 2 Kingston Lisle; 3 North Leigh. *Shropshire*: 1 Wroxeter. *Staffordshire*: 1 Wall. *Warwickshire*: 1 The Lunt, Baginton. *Wiltshire*: 1 Littlecote; 2 Rotherley and Berwick Down.

184

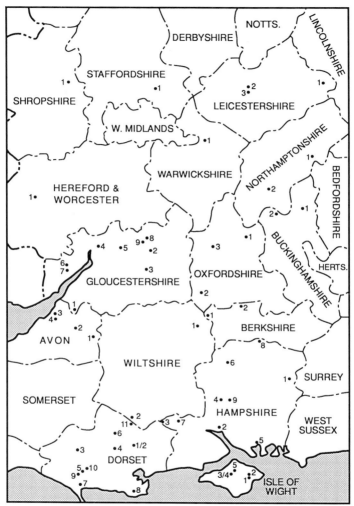

MAP 2.

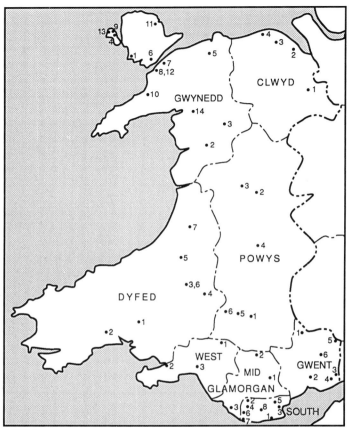

MAP 3.

Clwyd: 1 Ffrith; 2 Pentre; 3 Prestatyn; 4 Roman road. *Dyfed*: 1 Carmarthen; 2 Cwm Brwyn; 3 Dolaucothi; 4 Llandovery; 5 Llanio; 6 Pumpsaint; 7 Trawscoed. *Mid Glamorgan*: 1 Gelligaer; 2 Penydarren; 3 Ty Bryn. *South Glamorgan*: 1 Barry; 2 Cae Summerhouse; 3 Cardiff; 4 Cowbridge; 5 Ely; 6 Llantwit Major; 7 New Mill Farm; 8 Whitton. *West Glamorgan*: 1 Coelbren; 2 Loughor; 3 Neath. *Gwent*: 1 Abergavenny; 2 Caerleon; 3 Caerwent; 4 Caldicot; 5 Hardnock Farm; 6 Usk. *Gwynedd*: 1 Aberffraw; 2 Brithdir; 3 Caer Gai; 4 Caer Gybi; 5 Caerhun; 6 Caer Leb; 7 Caer Metta; 8 Caernarvon; 9 Caer-y-twr; 10 Cefn Graeanog; 11 Din Lligwy; 12 Hen Waliau; 13 Holyhead Mountain; 14 Tomen-y-Mur. *Powys*: 1 Brecon Gaer; 2 Caersws; 3 Carno; 4 Castell Collen; 5 Sarn Helen; 6 Y Pigwn.

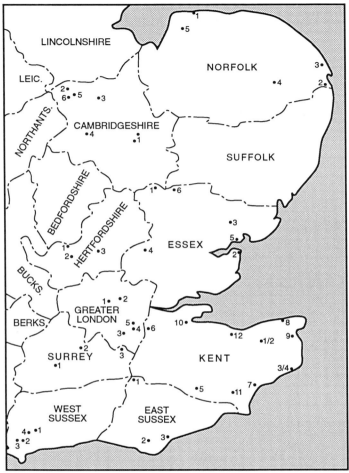

MAP 4.

Cambridgeshire: 1 Car Dyke; 2 Castor; 3 Chesterton; 4 Great Stukeley; 5 Orton Longueville; 6 Water Newton. *Essex*: 1 Bartlow Hills; 2 Bradwell; 3 Colchester; 4 Harlow; 5 Mersea Mount; 6 Sturmer. *Hertfordshire*: 1 Harpenden; 2 St Albans; 3 Welwyn. *Kent*: 1 Canterbury; 2 Canterbury, St Martin's church; 3 Dover, forts and Painted House; 4 Dover, lighthouse; 5 Iden Green; 6 Lullingstone; 7 Lympne; 8 Reculver; 9 Richborough; 10 Rochester; 11 Snargate; 12 Stone-by-Faversham. *Greater London*: 1 London; 2 Greenwich Park; 3 Keston; 4 Orpington, building; 5 Orpington, bath-house. *Norfolk*: 1 Brancaster; 2 Burgh Castle; 3 Caister-by-Yarmouth; 4 Caistor-by-Norwich; 5 Peddar's Way, Fring. *Surrey*: 1 Farley Heath; 2 Stane Street; 3 Titsey Park. *East Sussex*: 1 Holtye; 2 Long Man of Wilmington; 3 Pevensey Castle. *West Sussex*: 1 Bignor; 2 Chichester; 3 Fishbourne, 4 Stane Street.

187

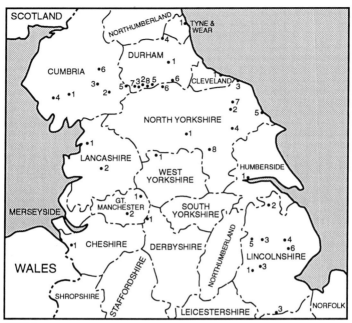

MAP 5.

Cheshire: 1 Chester. *Cleveland*: 1 Huntcliff. *Cumbria*: 1 Ambleside; 2 Crosby
Garrett; 3 Ewe Close; 4 Hardknott; 5 Maiden Castle, Stainmore; 6 Temple Sowerby.
Derbyshire: 1 Melandra Castle. *Durham*: 1 Binchester; 2 Bowes, fort; 3 Bowes,
signal station; 4 Ebchester; 5 Greta Bridge; 6 Piercebridge; 7 Rey Cross; 8 Scargill.
Humberside: 1 Brough-on-Humber. *Lancashire*: 1 Lancaster; 2 Ribchester. *Lincolnshire*: 1 Ancaster; 2 Caistor; 3 Car Dyke; 4 Horncastle; 5 Lincoln; 6 Revesby
Barrows. *Greater Manchester*: 1 Castleshaw; 2 Manchester. *Tyne and Wear*: 1
South Shields. *North Yorkshire*: 1 Aldborough; 2 Cawthorn; 3 Goldsborough; 4
Malton; 5 Scarborough; 6 Stanwick; 7 Wade's Causeway; 8 York. *West Yorkshire*:
1 Ilkley.

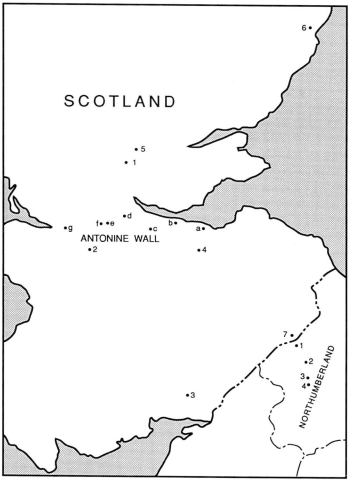

MAP 6.

Northumberland: 1 Chew Green; 2 High Rochester; 3 Risingham; 4 Swine Hill. *Antonine Wall*: a Cramond; b Kinneil Estate, Bo'ness; c Watling Lodge; d Rough Castle; e Croy Hill; f Bar Hill; g Bearsden. *Other Scottish sites*: 1 Ardoch; 2 Bothwellhaugh; 3 Burnswark; 4 Castle Greg; 5 Parkneuk; 6 Raedykes; 7 Woden Law and Pennymuir.

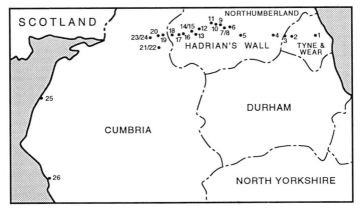

MAP 7.
Hadrian's Wall: 1 Wallsend; 2 Benwell; 3 Denton; 4 Heddon on the Wall; 5 Corbridge; 6 Brunton; 7 Chesters, bridge abutment; 8 Chesters, fort; 9 Black Carts; 10 Limestone Corner; 11 Carrawburgh; 12 Housesteads; 13 Chesterholm; 14 Castle Nick; 15 Winshiels; 16 Cawfields; 17 Greatchesters; 18 Carvoran; 19 Willowford; 20 Birdoswald; 21 Appletree; 22 Coombe Crag; 23 Banks East; 24 Banks Burn; 25 Maryport; 26 Ravenglass.

Index

Page numbers in italic refer to illustrations

190